APPLYING GOD'S WORD MORE FULLY

The Secret of a Successful Christian Life

Edward D. Andrews

—SECOND EDITION—

APPLYING GOD'S WORD MORE FULLY

The Secret of a Successful Christian Life

Second Edition

Edward D. Andrews

Christian Publishing House
Cambridge, Ohio

Copyright © 2016, 2024 Edward D. Andrews

All rights reserved. Except for brief quotations in articles, other publications, book reviews, and blogs, no part of this book may be reproduced in any manner without prior written permission from the publishers. For information, write, support@christianpublishers.org

APPLYING GOD'S WORD MORE FULLY: The Secret of a Successful Christian Life by Edward D. Andrews

ISBN-13: 978-1-945757-21-1

ISBN-10: 1-945757-21-3

Table of Contents

Preface 6
Introduction 8
CHAPTER 1 What Does It Mean to Apply God's Word Fully? 10
CHAPTER 2 Developing a Heart for God's Word 17
CHAPTER 3 The Power of Prayerful Bible Study 24
CHAPTER 4 Understanding the Conflict Between Two Natures 30
CHAPTER 5 Overcoming Spiritual Obstacles 36
CHAPTER 6 Renewing Your Mind Through Scripture ... 43
CHAPTER 7 Living Out the Moral Law Written on Your Heart 50
CHAPTER 8 Building a Personal Relationship with God 57
CHAPTER 9 Transforming Your Life Through Biblical Principles 65
CHAPTER 10 How Can We Find Peace in a World of Anxiety? 72
CHAPTER 11 Cultivating Joy and Contentment in Christ 79
CHAPTER 12 Practical Steps for Daily Scripture Application 85
CHAPTER 13 Maintaining Spiritual Growth Over the Long Term 92
CHAPTER 14 Understanding the Holy Spirit and Salvation 99

Edward D. Andrews

Preface

In a world filled with constant distractions, challenges, and conflicting messages, the need for a clear and unwavering guide to living a successful Christian life has never been more urgent. This book, *APPLYING GOD'S WORD MORE FULLY: The Secret of a Successful Christian Life,* is born out of a deep conviction that the Scriptures, when fully applied, hold the key to not only surviving but thriving in our spiritual journey.

The Christian life is not merely about intellectual assent to biblical truths; it is a life that demands action, transformation, and a continual striving toward the standards set forth by Jehovah in His Word. The purpose of this book is to equip believers with the tools and insights necessary to take those truths and apply them daily, in every aspect of their lives.

Throughout the chapters, you will find a comprehensive exploration of what it means to live in accordance with the Word of God. Each chapter is designed to delve into the practical application of Scripture, ensuring that the principles of the Bible are not just understood but are lived out in a way that brings about true spiritual growth and maturity. From developing a heart for God's Word to overcoming the inevitable spiritual obstacles, every aspect of the Christian walk is addressed with a focus on actionable steps grounded in Scripture.

This book is not for the passive reader. It is for those who are serious about their faith and are willing to put in the effort to deepen their relationship with Jehovah. It is for those who recognize that a successful Christian life is not achieved by accident but through deliberate and consistent application of God's Word.

As you embark on this journey through the pages of this book, my prayer is that you will be challenged, encouraged, and, most importantly, transformed. May the insights and truths contained within lead you to a more profound commitment to applying God's Word more fully in your life, for it is in this application that the true secret to a successful Christian life is found.

Edward D. Andrews

Author of 220+ books and Chief Translator of the Updated American Standard Version (UASV)

Edward D. Andrews

Introduction

The journey of faith is one marked by constant growth, challenge, and discovery. As Christians, we are called not just to believe in the Word of God but to live it out in every aspect of our lives. Yet, in the hustle and bustle of daily life, the application of Scripture can often feel daunting or even elusive. How do we take the ancient, divinely inspired words and make them relevant to our modern-day challenges? How can we ensure that our faith is not merely theoretical but practical, transformative, and deeply rooted in the reality of our everyday existence?

This book, *APPLYING GOD'S WORD MORE FULLY: The Secret of a Successful Christian Life,* is an invitation to embark on a journey of genuine transformation. It is a guide for those who desire to see the power of God's Word at work in their lives—not just in moments of crisis but in the quiet, ordinary rhythms of daily living. The secret to a successful Christian life is not hidden in obscure knowledge or lofty spiritual experiences; it is found in the simple, yet profound, act of applying God's Word fully and consistently.

Each chapter in this book is crafted to address specific areas of life where Scripture can and should be applied. From understanding the conflict between our old and new natures to building a personal relationship with Jehovah, this book provides practical strategies for aligning our lives with the truths of Scripture. The goal is to move beyond surface-level engagement with the Bible and into a deeper, more intentional practice of living out its teachings.

This journey is not about perfection, but about progress. It is about taking deliberate steps each day to apply the truths of God's Word, knowing that every effort, no matter how small, contributes to our growth in Christ. Whether you are a new believer or have been walking with the Lord for many years, the principles laid out in this book are designed to meet you where you are and help you take the next step in your spiritual journey.

APPLYING GOD'S WORD MORE FULLY

As you read, reflect, and implement the strategies discussed in these pages, remember that spiritual growth is a lifelong process. It requires perseverance, patience, and, above all, reliance on the grace of God. But as you commit to applying His Word more fully in your life, you will discover the profound joy, peace, and fulfillment that comes from living in accordance with His will.

Edward D. Andrews

CHAPTER 1 What Does It Mean to Apply God's Word Fully?

Understanding the Call to Apply God's Word Fully

To apply God's Word fully is to engage in a lifelong pursuit of living according to the principles, teachings, and commandments found within the Scriptures. This application is not merely an intellectual exercise or a passive acceptance of biblical truths; rather, it involves an active, deliberate effort to align one's life with the will of Jehovah as revealed in His Word. James 1:22 instructs us to "be doers of the word, and not hearers only, deceiving yourselves." This verse encapsulates the essence of what it means to apply God's Word fully. It's about moving beyond mere acknowledgment of Scripture to integrating its teachings into every aspect of our lives.

The process of applying God's Word involves more than just external conformity to biblical standards; it requires an internal transformation that shapes our thoughts, attitudes, and actions. This transformation is brought about by a renewed mind, as Romans 12:2 states: "And do not be conformed to this world, but be transformed by the renewal of your mind, that by testing you may discern what is the will of God, what is good and acceptable and perfect." The renewal of the mind is central to applying God's Word fully because it is through a renewed mind that we are able to discern and understand God's will and then act upon it.

The Necessity of Heartfelt Obedience

Applying God's Word fully requires heartfelt obedience, which means obeying not just outwardly but from the heart. Jesus emphasized this in Matthew 15:8-9 when He quoted Isaiah, saying, "This people honors me with their lips, but their heart is far from me; in vain do they worship me, teaching as doctrines the commandments of men." True obedience to God is not about performing religious rituals or following human traditions but about sincerely aligning our hearts and lives with His Word.

Heartfelt obedience is demonstrated by a willingness to submit to God's authority in all things, even when it is difficult or when it goes against our natural inclinations. For example, Jesus taught in Luke 6:27-28, "But I say to you who hear, Love your enemies, do good to those who hate you, bless those who curse you, pray for those who abuse you." This command challenges our natural tendencies, yet it is a clear example of what it means to apply God's Word fully—choosing to obey God's commands even when it is counterintuitive or uncomfortable.

The Role of Prayer in Applying God's Word

Prayer plays a crucial role in the application of God's Word. It is through prayer that we seek God's guidance, strength, and wisdom to live according to His Word. Philippians 4:6-7 encourages us, saying, "Do not be anxious about anything, but in everything by prayer and supplication with thanksgiving let your requests be made known to God. And the peace of God, which surpasses all understanding, will guard your hearts and your minds in Christ Jesus." Prayer is not just a means of communicating with God; it is also a way to align our will with His and to invite His power to work in our lives as we strive to apply His Word fully.

However, prayer must be coupled with action. James 2:26 tells us that "faith apart from works is dead." If we pray for God's help in overcoming a particular sin or in growing in a certain area, we must also take practical steps toward that goal. For instance, if one is praying for patience, it is essential to actively practice patience in daily situations. If someone is praying for a deeper understanding of Scripture, they must also commit to regular study of the Bible. In this way, prayer and action work together to help us apply God's Word fully.

The Impact of God's Word on Our Daily Decisions

One of the most significant aspects of applying God's Word fully is allowing it to influence our daily decisions. Proverbs 3:5-6 advises, "Trust in Jehovah with all your heart, and do not lean on your own understanding. In all your ways acknowledge him, and he will make straight your paths." This passage underscores the importance of seeking God's guidance in every decision we make. Whether it is in our personal relationships, our work, or our financial decisions, we must constantly ask ourselves how our choices align with biblical principles.

The Word of God provides wisdom for every aspect of life. For example, in financial matters, Proverbs 22:7 warns, "The rich rules over the poor, and the borrower is the slave of the lender." This verse reminds us of the dangers of debt and encourages us to live within our means. In our relationships, Ephesians 4:32 instructs, "Be kind to one another, tenderhearted, forgiving one another, as God in Christ forgave you." This principle of forgiveness is essential for maintaining healthy relationships and is a direct application of God's Word in our daily interactions.

Cultivating a Lifestyle of Obedience

Applying God's Word fully is not a one-time event but a continuous process that requires diligence and perseverance. Deuteronomy 6:6-7 emphasizes the importance of constant engagement with Scripture: "And these words that I command you today shall be on your heart. You shall teach them diligently to your children, and shall talk of them when you sit in your house, and when you walk by the way, and when you lie down, and when you rise." This passage highlights the need to integrate God's Word into every aspect of our lives, making it the foundation of our daily routines and conversations.

To cultivate a lifestyle of obedience, it is crucial to develop habits that reinforce the application of God's Word. Regular Bible study, prayer, and fellowship with other believers are essential practices that help us stay grounded in Scripture and encourage us to live according to its teachings. Hebrews 10:24-25 reminds us, "And let us consider how to stir up one another to love and good works, not neglecting to meet together, as is the habit of some, but encouraging one another, and all the more as you see the Day drawing near." Fellowship with other believers provides accountability and support as we seek to apply God's Word in our lives.

The Transformative Power of God's Word

The Word of God is not just a set of rules or guidelines; it is living and active, capable of transforming our lives. Hebrews 4:12 declares, "For the word of God is living and active, sharper than any two-edged sword, piercing to the division of soul and of spirit, of joints and of marrow, and discerning the thoughts and intentions of the heart." This verse highlights the dynamic nature of God's Word and its ability to penetrate our hearts and minds, revealing our true motives and leading us to genuine repentance and change.

As we apply God's Word fully, we will experience its transformative power in our lives. This transformation is not just about outward behavior but involves a deep, internal change that affects our character and our relationship with God. Colossians 3:10 speaks of this transformation, saying, "and have put on the new self, which is being renewed in knowledge after the image of its creator." The more we immerse ourselves in God's Word and apply it to our lives, the more we are conformed to the image of Christ, growing in holiness and righteousness.

Overcoming Challenges in Applying God's Word

While the benefits of applying God's Word fully are immense, it is not without challenges. One of the greatest obstacles we face is our own sinful nature. Romans 7:18-19 acknowledges this struggle: "For I know that nothing good dwells in me, that is, in my flesh. For I have the desire to do what is right, but not the ability to carry it out. For I do not do the good I want, but the evil I do not want is what I keep on doing." This passage resonates with the experience of many believers who find it difficult to consistently live according to God's Word.

To overcome these challenges, it is essential to rely on God's strength rather than our own. Philippians 4:13 reminds us, "I can do all things through him who strengthens me." This verse is a powerful reminder that our ability to apply God's Word fully comes not from our own efforts but from the strength and grace that God provides. Additionally, it is important to be patient with ourselves as we grow in our obedience. Proverbs 24:16 offers encouragement, saying, "for the righteous falls seven times and rises again, but the wicked stumble in times of calamity." The Christian life is a journey, and while we may stumble, we must continue to rise and press forward in our pursuit of living according to God's Word.

The Role of the Community in Applying God's Word

The Christian community plays a vital role in helping us apply God's Word fully. Ecclesiastes 4:9-10 teaches, "Two are better than one, because they have a good reward for their toil. For if they fall, one will lift up his fellow. But woe to him who is alone when he falls and has not another to lift him up!" This passage underscores the importance of fellowship and mutual support within the body of Christ. When we are part of a community of believers, we have the encouragement, accountability, and support we need to stay faithful to God's Word.

Moreover, the community provides a context in which we can practice the principles of Scripture. In the church, we have opportunities to love, serve, forgive, and bear with one another, as commanded in Colossians 3:12-14: "Put on then, as God's chosen ones, holy and beloved, compassionate hearts, kindness, humility, meekness, and patience, bearing with one another and, if one has a complaint against another, forgiving each other; as the Lord has forgiven you, so you also must forgive. And above all these put on love, which binds everything together in perfect harmony." The community is where the theoretical knowledge of Scripture becomes practical, lived-out reality.

The Eternal Significance of Applying God's Word

Finally, the application of God's Word has eternal significance. Jesus Himself emphasized the importance of obedience in Matthew 7:24-27, where He contrasts the wise man who built his house on the rock with the foolish man who built his house on the sand. "Everyone then who hears these words of mine and does them will be like a wise man who built his house on the rock. And the rain fell, and the floods came, and the winds blew and beat on that house, but it did not fall, because it had been founded on the rock. And everyone who hears these words of mine and does not do them will be like a foolish man who built his house on the sand. And the rain fell, and the floods came, and the winds blew and beat against that house, and it fell, and great was the fall of it."

This parable illustrates that the foundation of our lives must be built on obedience to God's Word. Only then can we withstand the trials and challenges of life and ultimately stand firm on the Day of Judgment. The choices we make in this life, whether to apply God's Word fully or not, will have consequences that extend into eternity. Revelation 22:12-14 further emphasizes this, where Jesus says, "Behold, I am coming soon, bringing my recompense with me, to repay each one for what he has done. I am the Alpha and the Omega, the first and the last, the beginning and the end. Blessed are those who wash their robes, so that they may have the right to the tree of life and that they may enter the city by the gates." Applying God's Word fully is not just about living a successful Christian life in the here and now; it is about preparing for the life to come.

Continuing the Journey of Faith

As we continue in our journey of faith, let us be diligent in applying God's Word fully, knowing that it is not by our might or power but by Jehovah's Spirit that we are enabled to do so. Zechariah 4:6 reminds us, "Not by might, nor by power, but by my Spirit, says Jehovah of hosts." As we seek to live according to God's Word, may we always rely on His grace, strength, and guidance, trusting that He who began a good work in us will bring it to completion at the day of Jesus Christ (Philippians 1:6).

Let the Word of God dwell richly in our hearts, guiding our thoughts, shaping our desires, and directing our actions, so that we may live lives that are pleasing to Him, bearing fruit in every good work, and growing in the knowledge of God (Colossians 1:10). In doing so, we will fulfill the high calling to which we have been called, and our lives will be a testimony to the transforming power of God's Word.

CHAPTER 2 Developing a Heart for God's Word

The Foundation of a Heart for God's Word: A Love for Jehovah

Developing a heart for God's Word begins with cultivating a deep love for Jehovah, the author of the Scriptures. The Bible is not merely a collection of ancient writings; it is the inspired Word of God, "profitable for teaching, for reproof, for correction, and for training in righteousness" (2 Timothy 3:16). To develop a heart for God's Word, one must first recognize that it is the primary means through which Jehovah communicates with His people, offering guidance, wisdom, and insight into His will.

Psalm 119:97 expresses this love beautifully: "Oh how I love your law! It is my meditation all the day." This verse illustrates that a genuine affection for God's Word is not just about intellectual understanding but involves a deep emotional connection to the Scriptures. It is the recognition that in His Word, Jehovah has provided us with the roadmap to living a life that is pleasing to Him. Our love for God and His Word should be the driving force behind our desire to study, understand, and apply the Bible in our daily lives.

The Role of the Heart in Biblical Understanding

In the biblical sense, the heart is not merely the seat of emotions; it is the center of our being, encompassing our thoughts, desires, and will. Proverbs 4:23 warns, "Keep your heart with all vigilance, for from it flow the springs of life." This verse highlights the importance of guarding our hearts because the condition of our hearts directly affects our ability to understand and apply God's Word.

A heart that is hardened by sin or distracted by worldly concerns will struggle to receive and retain the truths of Scripture. Jesus addressed this in the Parable of the Sower, where He described different types of soil representing different conditions of the heart (Matthew 13:3-9, 18-23). The seed that fell on good soil represents a heart that is open, receptive, and ready to accept God's Word. To develop a heart for God's Word, we must cultivate a heart that is like the good soil—one that is humble, teachable, and willing to be transformed by the truths of Scripture.

The Necessity of Humility in Approaching God's Word

Humility is a crucial aspect of developing a heart for God's Word. James 1:21 instructs, "Therefore put away all filthiness and rampant wickedness and receive with meekness the implanted word, which is able to save your souls." To receive God's Word with meekness means to approach it with a humble and teachable spirit, recognizing that we do not have all the answers and that we need Jehovah's guidance to navigate life's complexities.

The Pharisees in Jesus' time were knowledgeable in the Scriptures, yet their hearts were hardened by pride and self-righteousness, preventing them from recognizing the truth of Jesus' teachings (Matthew 23:27-28). In contrast, those who were humble and aware of their need for God's mercy were more receptive to His Word (Luke 18:13-14). A humble heart is open to correction and willing to submit to God's authority, even when it challenges personal beliefs or preferences.

Developing a Consistent Habit of Meditation on Scripture

To develop a heart for God's Word, it is essential to meditate on Scripture consistently. Meditation, in the biblical sense, involves more than just reading; it requires thoughtful reflection and a deep engagement with the text. Psalm 1:2 describes the blessed man as one whose "delight is in the law of Jehovah, and on his law he meditates day and night." This continuous meditation on God's Word nourishes the soul and allows the truths of Scripture to take root in our hearts.

Meditation on Scripture involves pondering its meaning, considering how it applies to our lives, and allowing its truths to shape our thoughts and actions. Joshua 1:8 emphasizes the importance of meditation: "This Book of the Law shall not depart from your mouth, but you shall meditate on it day and night, so that you may be careful to do according to all that is written in it. For then you will make your way prosperous, and then you will have good success." Meditation leads to a deeper understanding of God's Word and empowers us to live according to its precepts.

The Importance of Prayer in Developing a Heart for God's Word

Prayer is an essential component in developing a heart for God's Word. As we study the Scriptures, we must pray for understanding, wisdom, and the ability to apply what we learn. Psalm 119:18 is a powerful prayer: "Open my eyes, that I may behold wondrous things out of your law." This prayer acknowledges our dependence on Jehovah to illuminate His Word and to grant us insight into its meaning.

In addition to praying for understanding, we must also pray for the desire and discipline to study God's Word regularly. Psalm 119:36-37 expresses this desire: "Incline my heart to your testimonies, and not to selfish gain! Turn my eyes from looking at worthless things; and give me life in your ways." Prayer aligns our hearts with God's will and creates in us a hunger for His Word, enabling us to develop a deeper love and commitment to studying the Scriptures.

Overcoming Distractions and Obstacles to Engage with God's Word

In our modern world, distractions abound, making it challenging to focus on and engage with God's Word. Jesus warned about the dangers of distraction in the Parable of the Sower when He described the seed that fell among thorns, which were choked by the cares of the world and the deceitfulness of riches (Matthew 13:22). These distractions can prevent us from developing a heart for God's Word by diverting our attention away from what truly matters.

To overcome these distractions, we must be intentional about setting aside time to study and meditate on Scripture. This may require making sacrifices, such as turning off the television, limiting time on social media, or waking up earlier to spend time in the Word. Hebrews 12:1-2 encourages us to "lay aside every weight, and sin which clings so closely, and let us run with endurance the race that is set before us, looking to Jesus, the founder and perfecter of our faith." By eliminating distractions and focusing our hearts on God's Word, we can develop a deeper, more meaningful relationship with Jehovah.

The Role of the Holy Spirit in Illuminating God's Word

Although there is no indwelling of the Holy Spirit as taught by charismatic Christianity, the Holy Spirit does play a crucial role in illuminating God's Word and guiding believers into understanding the truths of Scripture. As we study the Bible, the Holy Spirit works through the Spirit-inspired Word of God to convict, instruct, and encourage us in our walk with Jehovah. Isaiah 11:2 describes the Spirit of Jehovah as "the Spirit of wisdom and understanding, the Spirit of counsel and might, the Spirit of knowledge and the fear of Jehovah." It is through the Spirit-inspired Word that we gain the wisdom and understanding necessary to apply God's Word fully.

As we study and meditate on Scripture, we should pray for the Holy Spirit's guidance to help us discern the meaning of the text and its application to our lives. Ephesians 1:17-18 reflects such a prayer: "that the God of our Lord Jesus Christ, the Father of glory, may give you the Spirit of wisdom and of revelation in the knowledge of him, having the eyes of your hearts enlightened, that you may know what is the hope to which he has called you, what are the riches of his glorious inheritance in the saints." Through the illumination of the Spirit-inspired Word, we can grow in our understanding of God's will and develop a heart that is fully devoted to Him.

Cultivating a Desire for Righteousness

A heart for God's Word is characterized by a desire for righteousness—a longing to live in a way that is pleasing to Jehovah. Jesus taught in Matthew 5:6, "Blessed are those who hunger and thirst for righteousness, for they shall be satisfied." This hunger and thirst for righteousness are evidence of a heart that has been transformed by the truths of Scripture and is committed to living according to God's standards.

To cultivate this desire for righteousness, it is essential to regularly examine our hearts and lives in light of God's Word. Psalm 139:23-24 offers a model for such self-examination: "Search me, O God, and know my heart! Try me and know my thoughts! And see if there be any grievous way in me, and lead me in the way everlasting!" By inviting Jehovah to search our hearts and reveal any areas of sin or disobedience, we can align our lives more closely with His will and grow in righteousness.

The Impact of Fellowship with Other Believers

Fellowship with other believers plays a significant role in developing a heart for God's Word. Hebrews 10:24-25 reminds us, "And let us consider how to stir up one another to love and good works, not neglecting to meet together, as is the habit of some, but encouraging one another, and all the more as you see the Day drawing near." Through fellowship, we are encouraged, challenged, and held accountable in our walk with Jehovah.

Being part of a community of believers provides opportunities to discuss and apply God's Word together. Acts 2:42 describes the early church as devoted "to the apostles' teaching and the fellowship, to the breaking of bread and the prayers." This model of community life emphasizes the importance of studying God's Word together and supporting one another in living out its truths. By engaging in regular fellowship, we can grow in our understanding of Scripture and develop a heart that is fully committed to Jehovah.

The Role of Worship in Developing a Heart for God's Word

Worship is another key element in developing a heart for God's Word. When we worship Jehovah, we acknowledge His greatness, sovereignty, and holiness, which deepens our reverence for His Word. Psalm 95:6-7 invites us, "Oh come, let us worship and bow down; let us kneel before Jehovah, our Maker! For he is our God, and we are the people of his pasture, and the sheep of his hand." Worshiping Jehovah in spirit and truth (John 4:24) helps to align our hearts with His and reinforces our commitment to living according to His Word.

Worship also provides a context in which we can reflect on the truths of Scripture and respond to them with praise and thanksgiving. Colossians 3:16 encourages us, "Let the word of Christ dwell in you richly, teaching and admonishing one another in all wisdom, singing psalms and hymns and spiritual songs, with thankfulness in your hearts to God." As we worship, the Word of God dwells more richly in our hearts, transforming our attitudes and actions to reflect His will.

The Importance of Obedience in Developing a Heart for God's Word

Obedience to God's Word is both a result of and a means to developing a heart for Scripture. Jesus emphasized the importance of obedience in John 14:15: "If you love me, you will keep my commandments." A heart that is committed to God's Word is one that not only hears but also obeys the teachings of Scripture.

James 1:22-25 provides a powerful exhortation to obedience: "But be doers of the word, and not hearers only, deceiving yourselves. For if anyone is a hearer of the word and not a doer, he is like a man who looks intently at his natural face in a mirror. For he looks at himself and goes away and at once forgets what he was like. But the one who looks into the perfect law, the law of liberty, and perseveres, being no hearer who forgets but a doer who acts, he will be blessed in his doing." Obedience to God's Word solidifies the truths of Scripture in our hearts and leads to spiritual growth and maturity.

The Long-Term Benefits of Developing a Heart for God's Word

Developing a heart for God's Word has long-term benefits that extend into eternity. Psalm 119:11 declares, "I have stored up your word in my heart, that I might not sin against you." By storing God's Word in our hearts, we are equipped to resist temptation and to live lives that are pleasing to Jehovah.

Moreover, a heart that is fully devoted to God's Word will experience the peace, joy, and fulfillment that come from walking in obedience to His will. Psalm 19:7-8 describes the blessings of living according to God's Word: "The law of Jehovah is perfect, reviving the soul; the testimony of Jehovah is sure, making wise the simple; the precepts of Jehovah are right, rejoicing the heart; the commandment of Jehovah is pure, enlightening the eyes." The more we immerse ourselves in Scripture and apply its truths to our lives, the more we will experience the abundant life that Jesus promised in John 10:10.

Finally, developing a heart for God's Word prepares us for the challenges and trials of life. When our hearts are anchored in Scripture, we can face difficulties with faith and confidence, knowing that Jehovah's Word provides the guidance and strength we need. Psalm 119:105 declares, "Your word is a lamp to my feet and a light to my path." By walking in the light of God's Word, we can navigate life's uncertainties with the assurance that He is with us, guiding our steps and leading us on the path of righteousness.

Edward D. Andrews

CHAPTER 3 The Power of Prayerful Bible Study

The Foundation of Prayer in Bible Study

Prayerful Bible study is essential for a believer seeking to apply God's Word more fully in their life. It combines the discipline of studying Scripture with the spiritual practice of prayer, creating a powerful synergy that deepens understanding and fosters spiritual growth. The Bible, as the inspired Word of God, provides the foundation for all aspects of Christian living, but to truly grasp its meaning and apply its teachings, prayer is indispensable.

James 1:5 states, "If any of you lacks wisdom, let him ask of God, who gives generously to all without reproach, and it will be given him." This verse emphasizes the need for prayer when studying Scripture, as it is Jehovah who grants the wisdom necessary to understand and apply His Word. Prayerful Bible study involves approaching the Scriptures with a heart that is open and receptive to God's guidance, asking Him to reveal the truths within His Word and to help us integrate them into our daily lives.

The Interconnection Between Prayer and Understanding

Understanding God's Word requires more than intellectual effort; it necessitates spiritual insight that only comes through prayer. The psalmist's plea in Psalm 119:18, "Open my eyes, that I may behold wondrous things out of your law," highlights the need for divine assistance in comprehending the depths of Scripture. Without prayer, our study of the Bible can become a purely academic exercise, lacking the transformative power that Jehovah intended.

Prayer invites the Holy Spirit to work through the Spirit-inspired Word, illuminating the Scriptures and revealing their application to our lives. Jesus promised in John 14:26, "But the Helper, the Holy Spirit, whom the Father will send in my name, he will teach you all things and bring to your remembrance all that I have said to you." While this promise was specifically to the apostles, it underscores the principle that God's Spirit works through His Word to guide believers into truth. In prayerful Bible study, we rely on this guidance to understand and apply the teachings of Scripture.

The Role of Prayer in Applying Scriptural Truths

Prayerful Bible study not only aids in understanding but also empowers us to apply the truths we discover. It is one thing to intellectually grasp a biblical principle; it is another to live it out in daily life. Romans 12:2 exhorts us, "Do not be conformed to this world, but be transformed by the renewal of your mind, that by testing you may discern what is the will of God, what is good and acceptable and perfect." This transformation and renewal of the mind occur as we pray over the Scriptures, asking God to help us not only understand His will but also to live according to it.

When we encounter challenging teachings in the Bible, such as Jesus' command to love our enemies (Matthew 5:44), prayer becomes crucial. Through prayer, we seek the strength and grace to live out these difficult commands, recognizing that without God's help, we are powerless to do so. Philippians 4:13 reminds us, "I can do all things through him who strengthens me." This strength comes through prayer, enabling us to apply God's Word in every area of our lives.

The Discipline of Combining Prayer with Scripture

Developing the discipline of combining prayer with Scripture is essential for spiritual growth. Just as regular Bible study is necessary for understanding God's Word, consistent prayer is vital for cultivating a relationship with Jehovah and for gaining the spiritual insight needed to apply the Scriptures. Colossians 4:2 urges believers to "continue steadfastly in prayer, being watchful in it with thanksgiving." This steadfastness in prayer, coupled with the study of Scripture, ensures that our hearts remain aligned with God's will.

One practical way to combine prayer with Bible study is through the practice of praying Scripture. This involves taking the words of Scripture and turning them into prayers. For example, when reading Psalm 51, which expresses David's repentance, we might pray, "Create in me a clean heart, O God, and renew a right spirit within me" (Psalm 51:10). This practice not only deepens our understanding of the text but also personalizes it, making the truths of Scripture more meaningful and applicable to our own lives.

The Transformative Power of Prayerful Reflection

Prayerful reflection on Scripture allows the Word of God to penetrate our hearts deeply, leading to lasting transformation. Psalm 119:11 declares, "I have stored up your word in my heart, that I might not sin against you." This storing up of God's Word is the result of meditative prayer, where we allow the Scriptures to dwell richly within us, shaping our thoughts, attitudes, and actions.

In prayerful reflection, we take time to ponder the meaning of the text, consider how it applies to our lives, and ask Jehovah to help us live according to its teachings. Joshua 1:8 emphasizes the importance of this practice: "This Book of the Law shall not depart from your mouth, but you shall meditate on it day and night, so that you may be careful to do according to all that is written in it. For then you will make your way prosperous, and then you will have good success." Through prayerful reflection, we internalize God's Word, allowing it to transform us from the inside out.

Overcoming Spiritual Obstacles Through Prayerful Study

Spiritual obstacles, such as doubt, temptation, and distraction, can hinder our ability to study and apply God's Word. Prayerful Bible study equips us to overcome these obstacles by strengthening our faith and focus. Ephesians 6:17-18 describes the Word of God as the "sword of the Spirit" and instructs us to pray "at all times in the Spirit, with all prayer and supplication." This imagery highlights the role of prayer in empowering us to wield God's Word effectively in spiritual battles.

When faced with doubt, prayer anchors us in the truth of Scripture. For example, when questioning God's goodness during times of suffering, we might turn to Psalm 27:13-14, which declares, "I believe that I shall look upon the goodness of Jehovah in the land of the living! Wait for Jehovah; be strong, and let your heart take courage; wait for Jehovah!" By praying through such Scriptures, we reaffirm our trust in Jehovah and find the strength to persevere.

Prayer as a Response to Biblical Revelation

Prayerful Bible study is not just about seeking understanding; it is also about responding to God's revelation in worship, thanksgiving, and obedience. As we study the Scriptures, we encounter the majesty, holiness, and love of Jehovah, which naturally leads to a response of worship. Revelation 4:11 proclaims, "Worthy are you, our Lord and God, to receive glory and honor and power, for you created all things, and by your will they existed and were created." In prayer, we echo this worship, praising God for who He is and for the truths revealed in His Word.

Thanksgiving is another important response to biblical revelation. Colossians 3:16-17 encourages us, "Let the word of Christ dwell in you richly, teaching and admonishing one another in all wisdom, singing psalms and hymns and spiritual songs, with thankfulness in your hearts to God. And whatever you do, in word or deed, do everything in the name of the Lord Jesus, giving thanks to God the Father through him." As we study the Scriptures, we are reminded of God's many blessings, and in prayer, we express our gratitude, cultivating a heart of thankfulness.

Obedience is the ultimate response to God's Word. James 1:22-25 warns, "But be doers of the word, and not hearers only, deceiving yourselves. For if anyone is a hearer of the word and not a doer, he is like a man who looks intently at his natural face in a mirror. For he looks at himself and goes away and at once forgets what he was like. But the one who looks into the perfect law, the law of liberty, and perseveres, being no hearer who forgets but a doer who acts, he will be blessed in his doing." Prayer empowers us to respond to God's Word with obedience, ensuring that our study of Scripture leads to practical application in our lives.

The Role of the Christian Community in Prayerful Bible Study

Prayerful Bible study is not meant to be a solitary activity; it is enriched by the involvement of the Christian community. Hebrews 10:24-25 emphasizes the importance of gathering together with other believers for mutual encouragement and support: "And let us consider how to stir up one another to love and good works, not neglecting to meet together, as is the habit of some, but encouraging one another, and all the more as you see the Day drawing near." By studying Scripture and praying together, believers can help each other grow in their understanding and application of God's Word.

In the early church, prayerful study of the Scriptures was a communal activity. Acts 2:42 describes the early Christians as devoted "to the apostles' teaching and the fellowship, to the breaking of bread and the prayers." This model of communal worship and study provides a powerful example for modern believers. By engaging in prayerful Bible study with other Christians, we benefit from their insights, are held accountable in our spiritual growth, and are encouraged to persevere in our faith.

The Long-Term Impact of Prayerful Bible Study

The long-term impact of prayerful Bible study is profound, leading to spiritual maturity, increased faith, and a closer relationship with Jehovah. 2 Timothy 3:16-17 highlights the purpose of Scripture: "All Scripture is breathed out by God and profitable for teaching, for reproof, for correction, and for training in righteousness, that the man

APPLYING GOD'S WORD MORE FULLY

of God may be complete, equipped for every good work." Prayerful study of the Bible equips believers for every aspect of Christian living, ensuring that they are fully prepared to serve Jehovah and to live according to His will.

As we continue to engage in prayerful Bible study, we will experience the ongoing transformation of our hearts and minds. Psalm 1:2-3 describes the blessedness of the one who delights in God's Word: "but his delight is in the law of Jehovah, and on his law he meditates day and night. He is like a tree planted by streams of water that yields its fruit in its season, and its leaf does not wither. In all that he does, he prospers." This imagery of a fruitful tree represents the spiritual vitality and prosperity that come from a life rooted in God's Word and nurtured by prayer.

In conclusion, prayerful Bible study is a powerful practice that transforms our understanding of Scripture, deepens our relationship with Jehovah, and empowers us to live out His Word in every area of our lives. By combining prayer with our study of the Bible, we invite Jehovah to speak to us through His Word, to guide us in truth, and to strengthen us to walk in obedience to His commands. As we continue in this discipline, we will grow in spiritual maturity and bear fruit that glorifies God.

CHAPTER 4 Understanding the Conflict Between Two Natures

The Origin of the Conflict: The Old Nature Versus the New Nature

The Christian life is marked by an ongoing struggle between two natures: the old nature, rooted in sin, and the new nature, birthed by the Spirit of God through the regenerative work of salvation. Understanding this conflict is crucial for every believer seeking to apply God's Word more fully in their life.

The apostle Paul vividly describes this conflict in Romans 7:21-23, where he writes, "So I find it to be a law that when I want to do right, evil lies close at hand. For I delight in the law of God, in my inner being, but I see in my members another law waging war against the law of my mind and making me captive to the law of sin that dwells in my members." This passage illustrates the internal battle every Christian experiences—the struggle between the desire to obey God and the inclination to follow sinful impulses.

The old nature, often referred to as the "flesh," is the remnant of the sinful tendencies inherited from Adam's fall (Romans 5:12). This nature is characterized by a propensity towards sin, rebellion against God's commands, and self-centeredness. In contrast, the new nature is created in the believer at the moment of salvation, as described in 2 Corinthians 5:17: "Therefore, if anyone is in Christ, he is a new creation. The old has passed away; behold, the new has come." This new nature reflects the character of Christ, embodying righteousness, holiness, and a desire to please God.

The Reality of the Struggle: A Daily Battle

The conflict between the old and new natures is not a one-time event but an ongoing, daily battle that persists throughout a Christian's life. Galatians 5:16-17 underscores this struggle: "But I say, walk by the Spirit, and you will not gratify the desires of the flesh. For the desires of the flesh are against the Spirit, and the desires of the Spirit are against the flesh, for these are opposed to each other, to keep you from doing the things you want to do." This opposition between the flesh and the Spirit is a constant reality for believers, requiring vigilance and reliance on God's grace to overcome.

The old nature seeks to reassert its influence, tempting the believer to revert to sinful habits, thoughts, and attitudes. This is why Paul exhorts believers in Ephesians 4:22-24 to "put off your old self, which belongs to your former manner of life and is corrupt through deceitful desires, and to be renewed in the spirit of your minds, and to put on the new self, created after the likeness of God in true righteousness and holiness." The process of putting off the old self and putting on the new self is not automatic; it requires intentional effort, discipline, and dependence on God's power.

The Role of the Mind in the Conflict

The mind plays a pivotal role in the conflict between the two natures. Romans 12:2 instructs believers, "Do not be conformed to this world, but be transformed by the renewal of your mind, that by testing you may discern what is the will of God, what is good and acceptable and perfect." The renewal of the mind is essential for overcoming the influence of the old nature and embracing the new nature in Christ.

The old nature is influenced by the world's values, which are often at odds with God's commands. This is why believers are warned in 1 John 2:15-16, "Do not love the world or the things in the world. If anyone loves the world, the love of the Father is not in him. For all that is in the world—the desires of the flesh and the desires of the eyes and pride of life—is not from the Father but is from the world." The world appeals to the old nature, enticing the believer to pursue sinful desires and worldly success.

In contrast, the new nature is nurtured by the truths of God's Word. Philippians 4:8 encourages believers to focus their minds on what is true, honorable, just, pure, lovely, commendable, excellent, and praiseworthy. By filling our minds with these things, we align our thoughts with God's will, strengthening the new nature and diminishing the influence of the old.

The Power of the Spirit in Overcoming the Old Nature

Victory in the conflict between the two natures is not achieved by human effort alone; it is made possible by the power of the Holy Spirit working through the Spirit-inspired Word of God. Romans 8:13 affirms this truth: "For if you live according to the flesh, you will die, but if by the Spirit you put to death the deeds of the body, you will live." The Holy Spirit empowers believers to put to death the sinful desires of the old nature and to live according to the new nature.

This process of sanctification—being made holy—is an ongoing work of the Spirit in the life of the believer. 2 Thessalonians 2:13 describes this work: "But we ought always to give thanks to God for you, brothers beloved by the Lord, because God chose you as the firstfruits to be saved, through sanctification by the Spirit and belief in the truth." The Spirit sanctifies us by revealing the truth of God's Word, convicting us of sin, and enabling us to live in obedience to God's commands.

It is important to note that while the Spirit empowers us to overcome the old nature, believers must cooperate with the Spirit by actively resisting temptation and pursuing righteousness. James 4:7 instructs, "Submit yourselves therefore to God. Resist the devil, and he will flee from you." Submission to God and resistance to the devil are essential components of living victoriously in the conflict between the two natures.

The Role of Scripture in Strengthening the New Nature

The Word of God is a powerful tool in the battle between the old and new natures. Hebrews 4:12 declares, "For the word of God is living and active, sharper than any two-edged sword, piercing to the division of soul and of spirit, of joints and of marrow, and discerning the thoughts and intentions of the heart." Scripture reveals the truth about our nature, exposes sin, and guides us in the path of righteousness.

Jesus Himself modeled the use of Scripture in resisting temptation during His time in the wilderness (Matthew 4:1-11). When confronted with the temptations of Satan, Jesus responded with Scripture, affirming the authority and power of God's Word. Believers are called to do the same, using Scripture to counter the lies of the enemy and to strengthen the new nature within them.

Psalm 119:11 emphasizes the importance of internalizing Scripture: "I have stored up your word in my heart, that I might not sin against you." By meditating on and memorizing God's Word, believers fortify their minds against the influence of the old nature and equip themselves to live according to the new nature. The regular study and application of Scripture are essential for spiritual growth and victory in the Christian life.

The Necessity of Prayer in the Battle Between the Natures

Prayer is another vital weapon in the believer's arsenal for overcoming the old nature and living according to the new. In Ephesians 6:18, after describing the armor of God, Paul urges believers to pray "at all times in the Spirit, with all prayer and supplication. To that end keep alert with all perseverance, making supplication for all the saints." Prayer connects us with Jehovah's power, enables us to resist temptation, and aligns our hearts with His will.

Prayer also plays a crucial role in seeking God's guidance and strength in the midst of the conflict between the two natures. Jesus taught His disciples to pray, "Lead us not into temptation, but deliver us from evil" (Matthew 6:13). This prayer acknowledges our dependence on God to help us avoid situations where the old nature might gain the upper hand and to deliver us from the schemes of the enemy.

Moreover, prayer helps us to maintain a close relationship with Jehovah, which is essential for spiritual victory. James 4:8 encourages us, "Draw near to God, and he will draw near to you." By staying close to God through prayer, we are better equipped to recognize and resist the influence of the old nature and to live according to the new nature in Christ.

The Importance of Community in the Conflict Between Natures

The Christian community plays a significant role in helping believers navigate the conflict between the old and new natures. Hebrews 10:24-25 highlights the importance of fellowship: "And let us consider how to stir up one another to love and good works, not neglecting to meet together, as is the habit of some, but encouraging one another, and all the more as you see the Day drawing near." Within the community of believers, we find encouragement, accountability, and support in our struggle against the old nature.

Fellow believers can provide wisdom, prayer support, and practical help in overcoming the challenges associated with the conflict between the two natures. Ecclesiastes 4:9-10 emphasizes the strength found in community: "Two are better than one, because they have a good reward for their toil. For if they fall, one will lift up his fellow. But woe to him who is alone when he falls and has not another to lift him up!" By engaging in meaningful relationships within the body of Christ, we strengthen our ability to resist the old nature and to live according to the new nature.

The Hope of Final Victory Over the Old Nature

While the conflict between the old and new natures is a persistent reality in the Christian life, believers have the assurance of final victory through Jesus Christ. Romans 7:24-25 expresses this hope: "Wretched man that I am! Who will deliver me from this body of death? Thanks be to God through Jesus Christ our Lord!" Although the battle continues in this life, we look forward to the day when we will be fully delivered from the presence of sin and the influence of the old nature.

This hope is rooted in the promise of glorification, the final stage of salvation, when believers will be completely conformed to the image of Christ and freed from the presence of sin. 1 John 3:2 proclaims, "Beloved, we are God's children now, and what we will be has not yet appeared; but we know that when he appears we shall be like him, because we shall see him as he is." The certainty of this future transformation motivates us to persevere in the battle between the two natures, knowing that our struggle is not in vain.

In conclusion, the conflict between the old and new natures is a central aspect of the Christian life. Understanding this struggle and applying God's Word more fully in the midst of it is essential for spiritual growth and victory. By relying on the power of the Holy Spirit, immersing ourselves in Scripture, maintaining a strong prayer life, and engaging in Christian community, we can overcome the influence of the old nature and live according to the new nature in Christ. As we do so, we move closer to the ultimate goal of being fully conformed to the image of our Lord and Savior, Jesus Christ.

CHAPTER 5 Overcoming Spiritual Obstacles

Understanding the Nature of Spiritual Obstacles

Every Christian faces spiritual obstacles that hinder their walk with Jehovah. These obstacles can take many forms, including temptation, doubt, fear, pride, and distractions. Understanding the nature of these obstacles is the first step in overcoming them. Spiritual obstacles are not merely external challenges; they often arise from within, rooted in the old nature that continues to exert influence over the believer.

Paul addresses the internal struggle with sin in Romans 7:18-19: "For I know that nothing good dwells in me, that is, in my flesh. For I have the desire to do what is right, but not the ability to carry it out. For I do not do the good I want, but the evil I do not want is what I keep on doing." This passage highlights the reality that spiritual obstacles often stem from the conflict between the old and new natures. Recognizing that these challenges are part of the Christian experience allows believers to approach them with the right mindset, seeking God's strength and guidance to overcome them.

The Role of Faith in Overcoming Obstacles

Faith is foundational in overcoming spiritual obstacles. Hebrews 11:1 defines faith as "the assurance of things hoped for, the conviction of things not seen." This assurance and conviction provide believers with the confidence to trust in Jehovah's promises and power, even when faced with seemingly insurmountable challenges.

One of the most significant examples of faith overcoming obstacles is found in the story of David and Goliath. David's faith in

Jehovah enabled him to confront and defeat the giant Goliath, despite the overwhelming odds (1 Samuel 17:45-47). David's faith was not in his own strength or abilities but in Jehovah, who had delivered him from danger in the past and whom he trusted to deliver him again. This story illustrates the principle that faith is not about self-reliance but about reliance on God, who is able to overcome any obstacle.

Jesus also emphasized the power of faith in overcoming obstacles. In Mark 11:22-24, He said, "Have faith in God. Truly, I say to you, whoever says to this mountain, 'Be taken up and thrown into the sea,' and does not doubt in his heart, but believes that what he says will come to pass, it will be done for him. Therefore I tell you, whatever you ask in prayer, believe that you have received it, and it will be yours." Faith in God's power and willingness to act on behalf of His people is crucial in overcoming the spiritual mountains that stand in our way.

The Importance of Prayer in Overcoming Obstacles

Prayer is an essential weapon in the battle against spiritual obstacles. Through prayer, believers access Jehovah's power, wisdom, and guidance, enabling them to overcome the challenges they face. James 5:16b reminds us, "The prayer of a righteous person has great power as it is working." Prayer is not just a ritualistic practice; it is a dynamic, powerful means of communication with God that brings about real change.

One of the key aspects of prayer in overcoming obstacles is the acknowledgment of our dependence on Jehovah. In 2 Chronicles 20:12, King Jehoshaphat faced an overwhelming enemy army and prayed, "O our God, will you not execute judgment on them? For we are powerless against this great horde that is coming against us. We do not know what to do, but our eyes are on you." This prayer exemplifies the humility and trust that should characterize our approach to spiritual obstacles. By acknowledging our weakness and relying on God's strength, we position ourselves to experience His deliverance.

In addition to praying for strength and guidance, believers should also pray for wisdom in navigating obstacles. James 1:5 encourages, "If any of you lacks wisdom, let him ask of God, who gives generously to all without reproach, and it will be given him." Spiritual obstacles often present complex challenges that require discernment and insight. By seeking God's wisdom through prayer, believers can make decisions that align with His will and avoid the pitfalls that hinder spiritual growth.

The Role of Scripture in Overcoming Obstacles

The Word of God is a powerful tool in overcoming spiritual obstacles. Hebrews 4:12 describes the Word of God as "living and active, sharper than any two-edged sword, piercing to the division of soul and of spirit, of joints and of marrow, and discerning the thoughts and intentions of the heart." Scripture not only reveals the nature of the obstacles we face but also provides the guidance and encouragement needed to overcome them.

When Jesus was tempted by Satan in the wilderness, He responded by quoting Scripture, saying, "It is written" (Matthew 4:1-11). By relying on the truth of God's Word, Jesus demonstrated the power of Scripture in resisting temptation and overcoming spiritual obstacles. Believers are called to follow His example by immersing themselves in God's Word and using it as a weapon against the enemy's schemes.

Psalm 119:105 declares, "Your word is a lamp to my feet and a light to my path." The guidance of Scripture is indispensable in navigating the spiritual obstacles that arise in the Christian walk. Whether facing temptation, doubt, or fear, the truths of Scripture illuminate the path forward, providing clarity and direction. By meditating on and memorizing Scripture, believers equip themselves to overcome obstacles and remain steadfast in their faith.

The Power of the Holy Spirit in Overcoming Obstacles

The Holy Spirit teaches and reminds us of God's commands, as illustrated in the Old Testament. Nehemiah 9:20 says, "You gave your good Spirit to instruct them and did not withhold your manna from their mouth and gave them water for their thirst." This verse highlights the instructional role of the Holy Spirit in guiding God's people. By immersing ourselves in Scripture, we allow the Holy Spirit to teach and remind us of God's truths, leading us to live in obedience.

The Spirit works through the Word of God to convict believers of sin, guide them into truth, and strengthen them in their battle against spiritual obstacles. John 16:8 states, "And when he comes, he will convict the world concerning sin and righteousness and judgment." This conviction is a crucial aspect of overcoming obstacles, as it leads to repentance and a renewed commitment to following God's commands.

The Holy Spirit also provides the power necessary to resist temptation and to live a life that is pleasing to Jehovah. Galatians 5:16 encourages believers to "walk by the Spirit, and you will not gratify the desires of the flesh." By walking in the Spirit, believers are empowered to overcome the obstacles that would otherwise lead them away from God's will.

The Role of Christian Fellowship in Overcoming Obstacles

Christian fellowship is another vital resource in overcoming spiritual obstacles. Ecclesiastes 4:9-10 emphasizes the importance of community: "Two are better than one, because they have a good reward for their toil. For if they fall, one will lift up his fellow. But woe to him who is alone when he falls and has not another to lift him up!" Believers are not meant to face spiritual challenges alone; they are part of the body of Christ, which provides support, encouragement, and accountability.

Hebrews 10:24-25 further underscores the value of fellowship: "And let us consider how to stir up one another to love and good works, not neglecting to meet together, as is the habit of some, but encouraging one another, and all the more as you see the Day drawing near." Within the context of Christian fellowship, believers can share their struggles, receive counsel, and find the strength to persevere in their walk with Jehovah.

Fellowship also provides opportunities for mutual prayer, which is powerful in overcoming spiritual obstacles. Matthew 18:19-20 affirms, "Again I say to you, if two of you agree on earth about anything they ask, it will be done for them by my Father in heaven. For where two or three are gathered in my name, there am I among them." The combined prayers of believers, united in faith, have a profound impact in bringing about God's intervention and guidance in overcoming challenges.

Practical Steps for Overcoming Specific Spiritual Obstacles

Overcoming spiritual obstacles requires practical, actionable steps that are grounded in Scripture and supported by prayer and fellowship. Here are some specific examples:

Temptation: To overcome temptation, believers should follow the example of Joseph, who fled from Potiphar's wife when she tried to seduce him (Genesis 39:12). Fleeing from temptation involves avoiding situations, people, or environments that lead to sin. Additionally, memorizing Scripture that addresses the specific temptation can provide strength in moments of weakness, as Jesus demonstrated in His wilderness temptations.

Doubt: When faced with doubt, believers can turn to the example of Thomas, who struggled to believe in Jesus' resurrection until he saw the evidence for himself (John 20:24-29). Jesus did not condemn Thomas for his doubt but provided the evidence he needed to believe. Believers should seek answers to their doubts through prayer, Scripture, and godly counsel, trusting that God will provide the assurance they need.

Fear: Overcoming fear involves trusting in God's sovereignty and promises. Psalm 56:3 declares, "When I am afraid, I put my trust in you." Believers can combat fear by focusing on God's faithfulness and recalling past instances where He has provided protection and deliverance. Prayer and Scripture meditation are key tools in replacing fear with faith.

Pride: Pride is a spiritual obstacle that often leads to a fall. Proverbs 16:18 warns, "Pride goes before destruction, and a haughty spirit before a fall." To overcome pride, believers must cultivate humility, as Jesus taught in Matthew 23:12: "Whoever exalts himself will be humbled, and whoever humbles himself will be exalted." This involves recognizing one's dependence on God, serving others selflessly, and regularly confessing and repenting of prideful attitudes.

Distraction: In a world full of distractions, staying focused on God and His Word can be challenging. Jesus addressed this issue in the Parable of the Sower, where He described the seed that fell among thorns, representing those who hear the Word but are choked by the cares of the world and the deceitfulness of riches (Matthew 13:22). To overcome distraction, believers must prioritize their relationship with Jehovah, setting aside time for prayer, Bible study, and fellowship, and avoiding activities that detract from their spiritual growth.

The Importance of Perseverance in Overcoming Obstacles

Perseverance is essential in overcoming spiritual obstacles. James 1:12 encourages believers, "Blessed is the man who remains steadfast under trial, for when he has stood the test he will receive the crown of life, which God has promised to those who love him." Perseverance involves remaining faithful to God and His Word, even when faced with difficulties and challenges.

The apostle Paul exemplified perseverance in his ministry, enduring persecution, imprisonment, and hardship for the sake of the gospel. In 2 Timothy 4:7, he writes, "I have fought the good fight, I have finished the race, I have kept the faith." Paul's unwavering commitment to his calling, despite the obstacles he faced, serves as an inspiration for believers to persevere in their own spiritual journey.

Perseverance is not something believers must muster on their own; it is a gift from God, who strengthens and sustains His people. Philippians 1:6 reassures us, "And I am sure of this, that he who began a good work in you will bring it to completion at the day of Jesus Christ." Believers can trust that Jehovah, who initiated their faith, will also provide the grace and strength needed to persevere through every obstacle.

The Role of Hope in Overcoming Obstacles

Hope is a powerful motivator in overcoming spiritual obstacles. Romans 8:24-25 explains, "For in this hope we were saved. Now hope that is seen is not hope. For who hopes for what he sees? But if we hope for what we do not see, we wait for it with patience." The hope of eternal life, the resurrection, and the fulfillment of God's promises gives believers the courage to face and overcome the challenges of this life.

This hope is not wishful thinking but a confident expectation based on the character and promises of God. Hebrews 6:19 describes this hope as "a sure and steadfast anchor of the soul." When faced with spiritual obstacles, believers can cling to the hope that God is faithful to His Word and will ultimately deliver them from every trial.

Hope also empowers believers to look beyond their present circumstances and focus on the eternal rewards that await them. 2 Corinthians 4:17-18 encourages, "For this light momentary affliction is preparing for us an eternal weight of glory beyond all comparison, as we look not to the things that are seen but to the things that are unseen. For the things that are seen are transient, but the things that are unseen are eternal." This eternal perspective helps believers endure hardships and remain steadfast in their faith.

CHAPTER 6 Renewing Your Mind Through Scripture

The Biblical Mandate for Mind Renewal

The concept of renewing the mind is central to the Christian life. It involves a transformation in how we think, perceive, and understand the world, aligning our thoughts with the truths revealed in Scripture. This process is not a mere intellectual exercise; it is a deep, spiritual change that affects every aspect of our lives. The Apostle Paul captures this essential transformation in Romans 12:2: "Do not be conformed to this world, but be transformed by the renewal of your mind, that by testing you may discern what is the will of God, what is good and acceptable and perfect." Here, Paul emphasizes the importance of rejecting worldly patterns of thought and embracing a mindset shaped by God's Word.

The necessity of mind renewal stems from the fact that, before coming to faith in Christ, our thinking was dominated by the values and philosophies of the world. Ephesians 4:22-24 describes the process of shedding the old self and adopting the new: "to put off your old self, which belongs to your former manner of life and is corrupt through deceitful desires, and to be renewed in the spirit of your minds, and to put on the new self, created after the likeness of God in true righteousness and holiness." This renewal is not instantaneous but a lifelong process of sanctification, in which the believer's mind is continually shaped and refined by the truths of Scripture.

The Role of Scripture in Mind Renewal

Scripture plays an indispensable role in renewing the mind. As the inspired Word of God, the Bible contains the wisdom, guidance, and truth necessary for transforming our thoughts and attitudes. Hebrews 4:12 declares, "For the word of God is living and active, sharper than any two-edged sword, piercing to the division of soul and of spirit, of joints and of marrow, and discerning the thoughts and intentions of the heart." The Word of God penetrates deeply into our innermost being, revealing areas that need to be brought into alignment with God's will.

The process of renewing the mind through Scripture involves several key practices. First, it requires regular and consistent reading of the Bible. Psalm 1:2 describes the blessed man as one who "delights in the law of Jehovah, and on his law he meditates day and night." Meditation on Scripture is more than simply reading; it involves pondering its meaning, reflecting on its implications, and allowing its truths to sink deeply into our hearts. By immersing ourselves in the Word, we begin to think more like God thinks, viewing life through the lens of His eternal truths.

Second, renewing the mind involves memorizing Scripture. Psalm 119:11 states, "I have stored up your word in my heart, that I might not sin against you." Memorizing Scripture equips us with the truth we need to counteract the lies of the world and the deceit of the old nature. When faced with temptation, doubt, or fear, recalling and meditating on memorized Scripture can provide the strength and guidance needed to stay faithful to God's commands.

The Impact of Mind Renewal on Behavior and Character

Renewing the mind through Scripture is not an end in itself; it is meant to produce tangible change in our behavior and character. As our thoughts are aligned with God's Word, our actions will naturally follow. Proverbs 4:23 emphasizes the importance of the mind-heart connection: "Keep your heart with all vigilance, for from it flow the springs of life." The condition of our hearts and minds directly influences the way we live. When our minds are renewed by Scripture, our lives will reflect the righteousness, holiness, and love that characterize the new nature in Christ.

The connection between mind renewal and behavior is further highlighted in Colossians 3:1-2: "If then you have been raised with Christ, seek the things that are above, where Christ is, seated at the right hand of God. Set your minds on things that are above, not on things that are on earth." Setting our minds on heavenly things involves focusing on the eternal truths of God's Word rather than the fleeting concerns of this world. As we do so, our priorities, values, and desires will be transformed, leading to a life that is increasingly conformed to the image of Christ.

The fruit of mind renewal is evident in the transformation of character. Galatians 5:22-23 lists the fruit of the Spirit as "love, joy, peace, patience, kindness, goodness, faithfulness, gentleness, self-control." These qualities are not produced by human effort but by the work of the Holy Spirit through the renewal of the mind. As our minds are saturated with Scripture, the Holy Spirit brings forth this fruit in our lives, enabling us to live in a manner that honors God and blesses others.

Overcoming Worldly Influences Through Mind Renewal

One of the primary reasons for renewing the mind is to overcome the pervasive influence of the world's values and philosophies. The world constantly bombards us with messages that are contrary to God's truth, promoting selfishness, materialism, and moral relativism. 1 John 2:15-17 warns, "Do not love the world or the things in the world. If anyone loves the world, the love of the Father is not in him. For all that is in the world—the desires of the flesh and the desires of the eyes and pride of life—is not from the Father but is from the world. And the world is passing away along with its desires, but whoever does the will of God abides forever."

Renewing the mind through Scripture enables us to resist these worldly influences by grounding our thoughts in eternal truths rather than temporary, earthly concerns. Romans 8:5-6 contrasts the mindset of the flesh with the mindset of the Spirit: "For those who live according to the flesh set their minds on the things of the flesh, but those who live according to the Spirit set their minds on the things of the Spirit. For to set the mind on the flesh is death, but to set the mind on the Spirit is life and peace." By focusing on the things of the Spirit, as revealed in God's Word, we can experience the life and peace that come from living in harmony with God's will.

The Role of Prayer in Mind Renewal

Prayer is an essential component of the mind renewal process. While Scripture provides the content for renewing the mind, prayer is the means by which we apply and internalize that content. Philippians 4:6-7 encourages believers, "Do not be anxious about anything, but in everything by prayer and supplication with thanksgiving let your requests be made known to God. And the peace of God, which surpasses all understanding, will guard your hearts and your minds in Christ Jesus." Prayer helps to guard our minds against anxiety, fear, and other negative thoughts, allowing the truths of Scripture to take root and bear fruit in our lives.

In addition to praying for peace and protection, believers should also pray for wisdom and understanding as they study Scripture. James 1:5 promises, "If any of you lacks wisdom, let him ask of God, who gives generously to all without reproach, and it will be given him." By seeking God's wisdom in prayer, we open ourselves to the guidance of the Holy Spirit, who illuminates the Scriptures and reveals how they apply to our lives.

Prayer also reinforces the truths we learn from Scripture, helping us to internalize them and make them a part of our everyday thinking. Colossians 3:16 encourages, "Let the word of Christ dwell in you richly, teaching and admonishing one another in all wisdom, singing psalms and hymns and spiritual songs, with thankfulness in your hearts to God." As we pray and meditate on Scripture, its truths dwell richly within us, shaping our thoughts, attitudes, and actions.

Practical Steps for Renewing the Mind

Renewing the mind is an ongoing process that requires intentional effort and discipline. Here are some practical steps for engaging in this process:

APPLYING GOD'S WORD MORE FULLY

Consistent Bible Reading: Regular, systematic reading of Scripture is foundational for mind renewal. By making Bible reading a daily habit, believers continually expose themselves to God's truth, allowing it to reshape their thinking.

Scripture Memorization: Memorizing key verses and passages enables believers to carry God's Word with them throughout the day, ready to combat negative thoughts and temptations with the truth.

Meditation on Scripture: Taking time to reflect deeply on specific passages helps to internalize God's Word, making it more than just information but a guiding principle for life.

Application of Scripture: Mind renewal is not complete until the truths of Scripture are put into practice. Believers should seek to apply what they learn from the Bible in their daily lives, whether in their relationships, work, or personal conduct.

Engagement in Christian Community: Fellowship with other believers provides encouragement, accountability, and support in the mind renewal process. Studying Scripture together and discussing its application helps to reinforce its truths and foster spiritual growth.

Prayerful Reflection: Combining prayer with Bible study allows believers to seek God's guidance in understanding and applying His Word. Prayer also provides a means of expressing dependence on God for the strength and wisdom needed to live according to His will.

The Challenges of Mind Renewal and How to Overcome Them

While the process of renewing the mind is essential for spiritual growth, it is not without challenges. Believers may encounter obstacles such as distractions, discouragement, and spiritual warfare that hinder their efforts to renew their minds through Scripture.

Distractions: In today's fast-paced, media-saturated world, distractions are everywhere, making it difficult to focus on God's Word. To overcome this challenge, believers must be intentional about setting aside time for Bible study and minimizing distractions during that time. This may involve turning off electronic devices, finding a quiet place to read, and prioritizing Bible study over other activities.

Discouragement: The process of mind renewal can be slow and difficult, leading to feelings of discouragement. Believers may struggle with old patterns of thinking that seem resistant to change. In such times, it is important to remember that mind renewal is a lifelong process that requires patience and perseverance. Galatians 6:9 encourages, "And let us not grow weary of doing good, for in due season we will reap, if we do not give up." Believers should continue in their efforts, trusting that God is at work in them, even when progress seems slow.

Spiritual Warfare: The enemy seeks to undermine the process of mind renewal by planting lies, doubts, and temptations in the believer's mind. Ephesians 6:12 reminds us, "For we do not wrestle against flesh and blood, but against the rulers, against the authorities, against the cosmic powers over this present darkness, against the spiritual forces of evil in the heavenly places." To combat these attacks, believers must rely on the full armor of God, including the "helmet of salvation" and the "sword of the Spirit, which is the word of God" (Ephesians 6:17). Prayer, Scripture, and reliance on the Holy Spirit are critical in standing firm against the enemy's schemes.

The Fruit of Renewed Minds

The ultimate goal of renewing the mind through Scripture is to become more like Christ in thought, character, and behavior. As believers engage in the process of mind renewal, they will begin to experience the fruit of the Spirit in greater measure, reflecting the character of Christ in their daily lives.

One of the most significant fruits of a renewed mind is the ability to discern God's will. Romans 12:2 explains that the renewal of the mind enables believers to "discern what is the will of God, what is good and acceptable and perfect." This discernment is not just about making decisions; it is about aligning one's entire life with God's purposes and priorities.

Another fruit of a renewed mind is the experience of God's peace. Philippians 4:7 promises, "And the peace of God, which surpasses all understanding, will guard your hearts and your minds in Christ Jesus."

APPLYING GOD'S WORD MORE FULLY

As believers renew their minds through Scripture, they learn to trust in God's sovereignty, wisdom, and love, resulting in a deep and abiding peace that transcends circumstances.

Finally, a renewed mind produces a life of greater holiness and righteousness. Ephesians 4:23-24 encourages believers to "be renewed in the spirit of your minds, and to put on the new self, created after the likeness of God in true righteousness and holiness." As the mind is transformed by Scripture, the believer's life will increasingly reflect the holiness of God, bringing glory to Him and drawing others to Christ.

In conclusion, the process of renewing the mind through Scripture is central to the Christian life. It involves a transformation in thought, character, and behavior that aligns believers with God's will and enables them to live in a way that honors Him. By engaging in regular Bible reading, meditation, prayer, and fellowship, believers can experience the ongoing renewal of their minds, leading to a life of greater faith, peace, and holiness.

Edward D. Andrews

CHAPTER 7 Living Out the Moral Law Written on Your Heart

The Origin of the Moral Law in the Human Heart

The concept of a moral law written on the human heart is rooted in the understanding that Jehovah, as the Creator, has embedded His moral standards within every individual. This innate sense of right and wrong is not merely a social construct but a reflection of God's righteousness imprinted on the human conscience. Romans 2:14-15 speaks to this truth: "For when Gentiles, who do not have the law, by nature do what the law requires, they are a law to themselves, even though they do not have the law. They show that the work of the law is written on their hearts, while their conscience also bears witness, and their conflicting thoughts accuse or even excuse them."

This passage highlights that even those who have not been exposed to the explicit teachings of the Mosaic Law possess an inherent understanding of moral principles. This moral awareness is a testament to the fact that God's law transcends written codes; it is an integral part of the human design, woven into the fabric of our being by our Creator. The moral law written on the heart serves as a guiding force, prompting individuals to act in ways that align with divine standards, even when they are not consciously aware of those standards.

The Role of Conscience in Moral Decision-Making

The conscience plays a crucial role in moral decision-making, serving as an internal compass that guides individuals in discerning right from wrong. The Bible consistently affirms the importance of a clear and pure conscience. Paul, in 1 Timothy 1:5, emphasizes the goal of Christian instruction: "The aim of our charge is love that issues from a pure heart and a good conscience and a sincere faith." A good conscience, aligned with the moral law written on the heart, is essential for living a life that pleases Jehovah.

However, the conscience is not infallible. It can be influenced, seared, or even corrupted by persistent sin, false teachings, or cultural norms that conflict with God's standards. 1 Timothy 4:2 warns of those "whose consciences are seared, as with a hot iron." This imagery suggests that repeated violation of one's moral awareness can lead to a dulled or insensitive conscience, making it difficult to discern right from wrong. Therefore, while the conscience is a vital tool for moral decision-making, it must be continually calibrated and informed by the Word of God to function correctly.

The Intersection of the Moral Law and Scripture

While the moral law is written on the human heart, Scripture provides the explicit, detailed articulation of God's moral standards. The Bible serves as the external authority that validates and clarifies the internal witness of the conscience. Psalm 19:7-8 captures the complementary relationship between God's Word and the moral law: "The law of Jehovah is perfect, reviving the soul; the testimony of Jehovah is sure, making wise the simple; the precepts of Jehovah are right, rejoicing the heart; the commandment of Jehovah is pure, enlightening the eyes."

Scripture not only affirms the moral law within but also expands upon it, offering specific commandments, principles, and examples that guide believers in righteous living. The Ten Commandments (Exodus 20:1-17) are a prime example of the moral law articulated in written form. These commandments reflect the moral principles inherent in every human heart, such as the prohibitions against murder, theft, and adultery. However, the written Word goes further by providing context, elaboration, and application of these principles, ensuring that believers understand how to live them out in every aspect of life.

The New Covenant and the Internalization of the Moral Law

The New Covenant, as foretold by the prophet Jeremiah and fulfilled in Christ, brings about a deeper internalization of the moral law. Jeremiah 31:33 prophesies, "For this is the covenant that I will make with the house of Israel after those days, declares Jehovah: I will put my law within them, and I will write it on their hearts. And I will be their God, and they shall be my people." Under the New Covenant, the moral law is not merely external; it becomes an integral part of the believer's identity and relationship with God.

This internalization is made possible by the regenerative work of the Holy Spirit through the Spirit-inspired Word of God, which transforms the heart and mind of the believer. Ezekiel 36:26-27 echoes this transformation: "And I will give you a new heart, and a new spirit I will put within you. And I will remove the heart of stone from your flesh and give you a heart of flesh. And I will put my Spirit within you, and cause you to walk in my statutes and be careful to obey my rules." The new heart, responsive to God's commands, is empowered to live out the moral law in a way that was impossible under the old, externalized covenant.

Living Out the Moral Law: A Life of Obedience and Love

Living out the moral law written on the heart involves more than mere compliance with rules; it is a life characterized by obedience to God and love for others. Jesus summarized the entire law in two commandments: "You shall love Jehovah your God with all your heart and with all your soul and with all your mind. This is the great and first commandment. And a second is like it: You shall love your neighbor as yourself. On these two commandments depend all the Law and the Prophets" (Matthew 22:37-40).

These two commandments encapsulate the essence of the moral law: love for God and love for others. Obedience to God flows naturally from a heart that loves Him. John 14:15 underscores this connection: "If you love me, you will keep my commandments." Love for God motivates believers to align their lives with His will, striving to live in a manner that honors Him and reflects His character.

Similarly, love for others is the practical outworking of the moral law in human relationships. Romans 13:8-10 explains, "Owe no one anything, except to love each other, for the one who loves another has fulfilled the law. For the commandments, 'You shall not commit adultery, You shall not murder, You shall not steal, You shall not covet,' and any other commandment, are summed up in this word: 'You shall love your neighbor as yourself.' Love does no wrong to a neighbor; therefore love is the fulfilling of the law." By loving others, believers fulfill the moral law and demonstrate the transformative power of God's grace in their lives.

The Role of the Holy Spirit in Empowering Obedience

While the moral law is written on the heart and articulated in Scripture, living it out requires the empowering work of the Holy Spirit. Philippians 2:12-13 emphasizes the believer's dependence on God's enabling power: "Therefore, my beloved, as you have always obeyed, so now, not only as in my presence but much more in my absence, work out your own salvation with fear and trembling, for it is God who works in you, both to will and to work for his good pleasure." The Holy Spirit works in believers to align their wills with God's will, enabling them to live in obedience to the moral law.

The Holy Spirit plays a crucial role in counseling, providing guidance, comfort, and conviction through the Spirit-inspired Word of God. We are guided when we act on behalf of our prayers by digging into the Scriptures and determining what the authors meant by the words they used. To illustrate, if we were praying for a job but never went out and filled out job applications, how would God feel about our prayers? If we were praying about the shame we feel over something, yet we never investigated what the Scriptures had to say about shame so as to apply them, how would Gold feel about our prayer?

Moreover, the Holy Spirit produces the fruit of the Spirit in the believer's life, which reflects the moral law in action. Galatians 5:22-23 lists this fruit: "But the fruit of the Spirit is love, joy, peace, patience, kindness, goodness, faithfulness, gentleness, self-control; against such things there is no law." These qualities are the embodiment of the moral law, manifesting in the believer's character and conduct as they yield to the Spirit's work.

Challenges in Living Out the Moral Law and How to Overcome Them

Living out the moral law written on the heart is not without challenges. Believers face internal and external obstacles that can hinder their obedience to God's commands. However, Scripture provides guidance on how to overcome these challenges.

Internal Challenges: One of the primary internal challenges is the ongoing struggle with the old nature, which is inclined toward sin Romans 7:21-23 describes this conflict: "So I find it to be a law that when I want to do right, evil lies close at hand. For I delight in the law of God, in my inner being, but I see in my members another law waging war against the law of my mind and making me captive to the law of sin that dwells in my members." To overcome this internal struggle, believers must rely on the Holy Spirit's power, as Romans 8:13 advises, "For if you live according to the flesh, you will die, but if by the Spirit you put to death the deeds of the body, you will live."

External Challenges: Believers also face external challenges from the world's values and pressures, which often conflict with God's moral standards. 1 John 2:16 warns, "For all that is in the world—the desires of the flesh and the desires of the eyes and pride of life—is not from the Father but is from the world." To resist these external pressures, believers must renew their minds through Scripture (Romans 12:2) and seek fellowship with other believers who encourage and support them in their walk with Christ (Hebrews 10:24-25).

APPLYING GOD'S WORD MORE FULLY

Persecution and Opposition: Living out the moral law can also lead to persecution and opposition, as Jesus warned in John 15:18-20: "If the world hates you, know that it has hated me before it hated you. If you were of the world, the world would love you as its own; but because you are not of the world, but I chose you out of the world, therefore the world hates you. Remember the word that I said to you: 'A servant is not greater than his master.' If they persecuted me, they will also persecute you." In the face of persecution, believers are called to remain steadfast, trusting in God's faithfulness and drawing strength from His promises.

Temptation: Temptation is another challenge that can hinder believers from living out the moral law. James 1:14-15 explains the nature of temptation: "But each person is tempted when he is lured and enticed by his own desire. Then desire when it has conceived gives birth to sin, and sin when it is fully grown brings forth death." To overcome temptation, believers must be vigilant in prayer (Matthew 26:41), resist the devil (James 4:7), and flee from situations that could lead to sin (1 Corinthians 10:13).

The Joy and Peace of Living According to the Moral Law

Despite the challenges, living according to the moral law written on the heart brings profound joy and peace. Psalm 119:165 declares, "Great peace have those who love your law; nothing can make them stumble." When believers align their lives with God's moral standards, they experience the peace that comes from a clear conscience and a life lived in harmony with God's will.

Furthermore, obedience to the moral law leads to a deeper relationship with God. Jesus promised in John 14:21, "Whoever has my commandments and keeps them, he it is who loves me. And he who loves me will be loved by my Father, and I will love him and manifest myself to him." As believers live out the moral law, they grow in their love for God and experience His presence in their lives in a more intimate and personal way.

In addition to peace and joy, living according to the moral law also brings blessings. Psalm 1:1-3 describes the blessedness of the person who delights in God's law: "Blessed is the man who walks not in the counsel of the wicked, nor stands in the way of sinners, nor sits in the seat of scoffers; but his delight is in the law of Jehovah, and on his law he meditates day and night. He is like a tree planted by streams of water that yields its fruit in its season, and its leaf does not wither. In all that he does, he prospers." Obedience to God's moral law leads to a fruitful and prosperous life, marked by spiritual growth and divine favor.

The Eternal Perspective of Living According to the Moral Law

Finally, living according to the moral law written on the heart has an eternal perspective. 1 John 2:17 reminds us, "And the world is passing away along with its desires, but whoever does the will of God abides forever." The choices believers make in living out the moral law have eternal significance, as they reflect their commitment to God's kingdom and their desire to honor Him in all things.

Living out the moral law is not about earning salvation or favor with God; it is the natural response of a heart that has been transformed by His grace. Ephesians 2:8-10 clarifies, "For by grace you have been saved through faith. And this is not your own doing; it is the gift of God, not a result of works, so that no one may boast. For we are his workmanship, created in Christ Jesus for good works, which God prepared beforehand, that we should walk in them." The moral law written on the heart guides believers in fulfilling the good works that God has prepared for them, works that bring glory to Him and have lasting value in His eternal kingdom.

In conclusion, living out the moral law written on the heart is a vital aspect of the Christian life. It involves a deep commitment to obedience, love for God and others, and reliance on the Holy Spirit's power. Despite the challenges and obstacles, the joy, peace, and eternal significance of living according to God's moral standards make it a worthy and fulfilling pursuit.

CHAPTER 8 Building a Personal Relationship with God

The Foundation of a Personal Relationship with God

A personal relationship with God is the cornerstone of the Christian faith. It is the foundation upon which every aspect of the believer's life is built, influencing thoughts, actions, and decisions. This relationship is not merely a religious formality but a dynamic, intimate connection with Jehovah, the Creator of the universe. In John 17:3, Jesus defines eternal life as knowing God: "And this is eternal life, that they know you, the only true God, and Jesus Christ whom you have sent." The word "know" in this context implies a deep, personal, and experiential knowledge, not just intellectual understanding.

This relationship begins with the recognition of God as our Father, a relationship made possible through the redemptive work of Jesus Christ. Romans 8:15-16 speaks of this new relationship: "For you did not receive the spirit of slavery to fall back into fear, but you have received the Spirit of adoption as sons, by whom we cry, 'Abba! Father!' The Spirit himself bears witness with our spirit that we are children of God." This passage highlights the intimate nature of the relationship, where believers are not only servants of God but His children, able to approach Him with the confidence and affection of a child toward a loving parent.

The Role of Faith in Building a Personal Relationship with God

Faith is essential in building and sustaining a personal relationship with God. Hebrews 11:6 asserts, "And without faith it is impossible to please him, for whoever would draw near to God must believe that he exists and that he rewards those who seek him." Faith is the means by which we come to know God and experience His presence in our lives. It involves trusting in God's character, promises, and provision, even when circumstances are challenging or unclear.

Abraham's relationship with God is a prime example of faith in action. In Genesis 15:6, it is recorded that "he believed Jehovah, and he counted it to him as righteousness." Abraham's faith was not a passive belief but an active trust that led him to obey God's commands, even when they required great sacrifice. This kind of faith is foundational for a personal relationship with God, as it involves surrendering our own will and desires in favor of God's plan for our lives.

Faith also involves believing in the truth of God's Word and allowing it to shape our relationship with Him. Romans 10:17 states, "So faith comes from hearing, and hearing through the word of Christ." As we immerse ourselves in Scripture, our faith is strengthened, and our understanding of God's character deepens, enabling us to build a more intimate relationship with Him.

Prayer as the Lifeline of a Personal Relationship with God

Prayer is the lifeline of a personal relationship with God. It is the means by which we communicate with our Heavenly Father, sharing our hearts, desires, fears, and joys with Him. Philippians 4:6 encourages believers to bring everything to God in prayer: "Do not be anxious about anything, but in everything by prayer and supplication with thanksgiving let your requests be made known to God." Prayer is not just about asking for things; it is about developing a deeper connection with God, aligning our hearts with His, and seeking His will in all things.

Jesus modeled the importance of prayer in maintaining a close relationship with God. In Mark 1:35, we see Jesus rising early in the morning to pray: "And rising very early in the morning, while it was still dark, he departed and went out to a desolate place, and there he prayed." If Jesus, the Son of God, needed to spend time in prayer, how much more do we, as His followers, need to cultivate this discipline?

Prayer is also a means of experiencing God's presence and power in our lives. James 5:16b reminds us, "The prayer of a righteous person has great power as it is working." Through prayer, we invite God to work in our lives, to transform our hearts, and to guide our steps. It is through consistent, heartfelt prayer that we grow in our relationship with God, learning to depend on Him in every aspect of life.

The Role of Scripture in Deepening a Personal Relationship with God

Scripture is God's primary means of revealing Himself to us. It is through the Bible that we come to know God's character, His will, and His ways. Psalm 119:105 declares, "Your word is a lamp to my feet and a light to my path." The Word of God illuminates the path of our relationship with Him, providing the guidance and wisdom needed to navigate life's challenges.

Regular, intentional study of Scripture is essential for deepening our relationship with God. 2 Timothy 3:16-17 emphasizes the importance of Scripture in the believer's life: "All Scripture is breathed out by God and profitable for teaching, for reproof, for correction, and for training in righteousness, that the man of God may be complete, equipped for every good work." As we engage with God's Word, we are taught, corrected, and trained in righteousness, equipping us to live in a way that honors Him and strengthens our relationship with Him.

Meditation on Scripture is another powerful way to deepen our relationship with God. Joshua 1:8 instructs, "This Book of the Law shall not depart from your mouth, but you shall meditate on it day and night, so that you may be careful to do according to all that is written in it. For then you will make your way prosperous, and then you will have good success." Meditating on Scripture involves reflecting on God's Word, allowing it to permeate our hearts and minds, and applying its truths to our lives. Through meditation, we internalize

God's Word, which draws us closer to Him and transforms our relationship with Him.

The Importance of Obedience in Building a Personal Relationship with God

Obedience is a crucial aspect of a personal relationship with God. Jesus made it clear that love for Him is demonstrated through obedience to His commands. John 14:15 states, "If you love me, you will keep my commandments." Obedience is not about legalism or earning God's favor; it is about aligning our lives with His will and walking in the way that He has set before us.

1 John 5:3 further emphasizes the connection between love and obedience: "For this is the love of God, that we keep his commandments. And his commandments are not burdensome." Obedience flows from a heart that loves God and desires to please Him. It is through obedience that we experience the fullness of our relationship with God, as we submit to His authority and trust in His wisdom.

Obedience also leads to greater intimacy with God. In John 15:14-15, Jesus tells His disciples, "You are my friends if you do what I command you. No longer do I call you servants, for the servant does not know what his master is doing; but I have called you friends, for all that I have heard from my Father I have made known to you." Obedience to God's commands brings us into a closer relationship with Him, where we are no longer just servants but friends who share in His plans and purposes.

The Role of Worship in a Personal Relationship with God

Worship is another vital component of a personal relationship with God. It is through worship that we express our love, adoration, and reverence for Jehovah. Psalm 95:6-7 invites us to worship God with humility and gratitude: "Oh come, let us worship and bow down; let us kneel before Jehovah, our Maker! For he is our God, and we are the people of his pasture, and the sheep of his hand." Worship is a response to who God is and what He has done, and it draws us closer to Him.

Worship also involves more than just singing songs or participating in church services; it is a lifestyle of honoring God in everything we do. Romans 12:1 encourages believers to offer their bodies as living sacrifices, holy and pleasing to God—this is our true and proper worship. Worshiping God in this way means living our lives in a manner that reflects His holiness and brings glory to His name.

Worship also serves to remind us of God's greatness and our dependence on Him. Psalm 100:4-5 instructs us to "Enter his gates with thanksgiving, and his courts with praise! Give thanks to him; bless his name! For Jehovah is good; his steadfast love endures forever, and his faithfulness to all generations." As we worship, we acknowledge God's goodness and faithfulness, which deepens our trust in Him and strengthens our relationship with Him.

The Role of Fellowship in a Personal Relationship with God

Fellowship with other believers is an important aspect of building a personal relationship with God. Christian fellowship provides encouragement, accountability, and support as we grow in our faith. Hebrews 10:24-25 emphasizes the importance of meeting together: "And let us consider how to stir up one another to love and good works, not neglecting to meet together, as is the habit of some, but encouraging one another, and all the more as you see the Day drawing near."

Through fellowship, we share our experiences, struggles, and victories with one another, which helps to strengthen our relationship with God. Proverbs 27:17 states, "Iron sharpens iron, and one man sharpens another." As we engage in fellowship, we sharpen one another, challenging each other to grow in our faith and to live out our relationship with God more fully.

Fellowship also provides opportunities for corporate worship, prayer, and study of God's Word, which are all essential for deepening our relationship with God. Acts 2:42 describes the early church's commitment to these practices: "And they devoted themselves to the apostles' teaching and the fellowship, to the breaking of bread and the prayers." This example serves as a model for how believers can strengthen their relationship with God through active participation in the community of faith.

The Role of Service in Building a Personal Relationship with God

Service is a natural outflow of a personal relationship with God. As we grow in our love for God, we are compelled to serve others in His name. Galatians 5:13 encourages believers to use their freedom to serve one another in love: "For you were called to freedom, brothers. Only do not use your freedom as an opportunity for the flesh, but through love serve one another." Service is an expression of our love for God and a way to reflect His character to the world.

Jesus Himself set the example of servant leadership, as seen in John 13:14-15: "If I then, your Lord and Teacher, have washed your feet, you also ought to wash one another's feet. For I have given you an example, that you also should do just as I have done to you." Serving others in humility and love not only strengthens our relationship with God but also demonstrates His love to those around us.

Service also helps to cultivate a deeper relationship with God by shifting our focus from ourselves to others. Philippians 2:3-4 instructs, "Do nothing from selfish ambition or conceit, but in humility count others more significant than yourselves. Let each of you look not only to his own interests but also to the interests of others." By serving others, we align our hearts with God's heart, which is characterized by selflessness, compassion, and a desire to bless others.

The Role of Trials in Deepening a Personal Relationship with God

Trials and difficulties are inevitable in the Christian life, but they also serve to deepen our relationship with God. James 1:2-4 encourages believers to view trials as opportunities for growth: "Count it all joy, my brothers, when you meet trials of various kinds, for you know that the testing of your faith produces steadfastness. And let steadfastness have its full effect, that you may be perfect and complete, lacking in nothing." Trials test and refine our faith, drawing us closer to God as we learn to rely on His strength and grace.

The apostle Paul also experienced the deepening of his relationship with God through trials. In 2 Corinthians 12:9-10, Paul shares how God's grace was sufficient for him in the midst of his weakness: "But he said to me, 'My grace is sufficient for you, for my power is made perfect in weakness.' Therefore I will boast all the more gladly of my weaknesses, so that the power of Christ may rest upon me. For the sake of Christ, then, I am content with weaknesses, insults, hardships, persecutions, and calamities. For when I am weak, then I am strong." Through trials, we experience God's sustaining power and grow in our trust and dependence on Him.

Trials also have the effect of purifying our faith and drawing us closer to God. 1 Peter 1:6-7 explains, "In this you rejoice, though now for a little while, if necessary, you have been grieved by various trials, so that the tested genuineness of your faith—more precious than gold that perishes though it is tested by fire—may be found to result in praise and glory and honor at the revelation of Jesus Christ." As we endure trials, our faith is refined, and our relationship with God is strengthened, leading to greater spiritual maturity and intimacy with Him.

The Joy of a Personal Relationship with God

The ultimate joy of the Christian life is found in a personal relationship with God. Psalm 16:11 proclaims, "You make known to me the path of life; in your presence there is fullness of joy; at your right hand are pleasures forevermore." The joy that comes from knowing God surpasses any earthly pleasure, as it is rooted in the eternal, unchanging nature of God's love and grace.

This joy is not dependent on circumstances but is a result of being in right relationship with God. Nehemiah 8:10 reminds us, "The joy of Jehovah is your strength." As we cultivate our relationship with God through faith, prayer, Scripture, worship, fellowship, service, and enduring trials, we experience the fullness of joy that comes from being in His presence and living according to His will.

In conclusion, building a personal relationship with God is the essence of the Christian life. It involves a deep, intimate connection with Jehovah, characterized by faith, prayer, obedience, worship, fellowship, service, and perseverance through trials. As we pursue this relationship with all our hearts, we will experience the fullness of life and joy that God has promised to those who seek Him.

CHAPTER 9 Transforming Your Life Through Biblical Principles

The Nature of Biblical Transformation

The process of transformation is central to the Christian life, representing a fundamental shift in how believers think, act, and interact with the world. This transformation is not merely a change in behavior but a profound reorientation of the heart and mind towards God. Romans 12:2 captures this idea succinctly: "Do not be conformed to this world, but be transformed by the renewal of your mind, that by testing you may discern what is the will of God, what is good and acceptable and perfect." This verse underscores the transformative power of renewing the mind through the application of biblical principles.

Biblical transformation involves moving away from the values and patterns of the world and embracing a new identity in Christ. This change is initiated by God through the Spirit-inspired Word and is an ongoing process that continues throughout the believer's life. As we delve into the Scriptures and apply its teachings, our lives are gradually conformed to the image of Christ, reflecting His character and values in every aspect of our existence.

The Foundation of Transformation: A New Identity in Christ

The foundation of any biblical transformation begins with understanding our new identity in Christ. When a person comes to faith in Jesus, they are given a new status before God—no longer sinners condemned under the law but children of God, redeemed and justified. 2 Corinthians 5:17 declares, "Therefore, if anyone is in Christ, he is a new creation. The old has passed away; behold, the new has come." This new identity is the basis for the believer's transformation, as it marks the beginning of a new life characterized by righteousness and holiness.

This transformation is rooted in the believer's union with Christ, as described in Romans 6:4: "We were buried therefore with him by baptism into death, in order that, just as Christ was raised from the dead by the glory of the Father, we too might walk in newness of life." Through faith, believers are spiritually united with Christ in His death and resurrection, symbolizing the end of the old self and the birth of a new creation. This new life is not merely a continuation of the old but a radical departure from it, marked by a desire to live according to God's will and purposes.

The Role of Scripture in Transforming the Mind

Scripture plays a crucial role in the transformation of the believer's mind. The Bible is not just a collection of ancient writings; it is the living and active Word of God, capable of penetrating the deepest parts of the human heart and revealing the thoughts and intentions within. Hebrews 4:12 states, "For the word of God is living and active, sharper than any two-edged sword, piercing to the division of soul and of spirit, of joints and of marrow, and discerning the thoughts and intentions of the heart."

By regularly reading, studying, and meditating on Scripture, believers allow God's Word to shape their thinking, replacing worldly perspectives with divine truth. Psalm 119:11 emphasizes the importance of internalizing Scripture: "I have stored up your word in my heart, that I might not sin against you." As the Word of God is internalized, it transforms the believer's desires, motives, and decisions, aligning them more closely with God's will.

One of the key principles of Scripture is the call to love God and love others. Jesus summarized the entire law in these two commandments: "And you shall love Jehovah your God with all your heart and with all your soul and with all your mind and with all your strength. The second is this: You shall love your neighbor as yourself. There is no other commandment greater than these" (Mark 12:30-31). This call to love forms the basis for the believer's transformation, as it encapsulates the essence of God's character and the life He desires for His people.

Applying Biblical Principles to Daily Life

The transformation of the believer's life through biblical principles involves more than just intellectual assent; it requires practical application. James 1:22-25 warns against being mere hearers of the Word, emphasizing the importance of putting it into practice: "But be doers of the word, and not hearers only, deceiving yourselves. For if anyone is a hearer of the word and not a doer, he is like a man who looks intently at his natural face in a mirror. For he looks at himself and goes away and at once forgets what he was like. But the one who looks into the perfect law, the law of liberty, and perseveres, being no hearer who forgets but a doer who acts, he will be blessed in his doing."

Applying biblical principles to daily life involves making conscious choices that reflect the teachings of Scripture. For example, the principle of forgiveness, as taught by Jesus in Matthew 6:14-15, is a powerful agent of transformation: "For if you forgive others their trespasses, your heavenly Father will also forgive you, but if you do not forgive others their trespasses, neither will your Father forgive your trespasses." Forgiveness is not just a passive response but an active decision to release others from the debt they owe us, reflecting God's forgiveness toward us.

Another principle is the call to humility, as taught in Philippians 2:3-4: "Do nothing from selfish ambition or conceit, but in humility count others more significant than yourselves. Let each of you look not only to his own interests but also to the interests of others." Humility transforms relationships by promoting selflessness and a willingness to serve others, mirroring the attitude of Christ, who "emptied himself, by taking the form of a servant" (Philippians 2:7).

Overcoming Obstacles to Transformation

The process of transformation is often met with resistance, both from within and without. The old nature, with its inclinations toward sin, does not easily surrender to the new life in Christ. Paul speaks of this ongoing struggle in Galatians 5:17: "For the desires of the flesh are against the Spirit, and the desires of the Spirit are against the flesh, for these are opposed to each other, to keep you from doing the things you want to do." This internal conflict can hinder the believer's progress in living out biblical principles.

To overcome these obstacles, believers must rely on the Holy Spirit's power, as described in Galatians 5:16: "But I say, walk by the Spirit, and you will not gratify the desires of the flesh." Walking by the Spirit involves a continual dependence on God's strength, seeking His guidance through prayer and Scripture, and allowing the Spirit-inspired Word to direct our thoughts and actions.

External obstacles also pose challenges to transformation. The values and pressures of the world often conflict with biblical principles, tempting believers to conform to the world rather than being transformed by the renewal of their minds. Romans 12:2 again offers the solution: "Do not be conformed to this world, but be transformed by the renewal of your mind." By resisting the allure of worldly values and focusing on God's truth, believers can remain steadfast in their commitment to living out biblical principles.

The Role of Community in Transformation

Christian community plays a vital role in the believer's transformation. The body of Christ, the church, provides the support, encouragement, and accountability needed to live out biblical principles. Hebrews 10:24-25 emphasizes the importance of gathering together: "And let us consider how to stir up one another to love and good works, not neglecting to meet together, as is the habit of some, but encouraging one another, and all the more as you see the Day drawing near."

Within the community of believers, individuals can share their struggles, receive counsel, and celebrate victories in their journey of transformation. Proverbs 27:17 highlights the mutual sharpening that occurs in Christian fellowship: "Iron sharpens iron, and one man sharpens another." This sharpening process helps believers to stay focused on their commitment to living out biblical principles, as they are challenged and encouraged by the example and testimony of others.

The church also provides opportunities for service, which is a crucial aspect of living out biblical principles. Ephesians 2:10 reminds believers that they are "created in Christ Jesus for good works, which God prepared beforehand, that we should walk in them." Serving others within the church and in the broader community not only reflects the love of Christ but also helps to solidify the transformation that is taking place in the believer's life.

The Fruit of a Transformed Life

The ultimate evidence of a life transformed by biblical principles is the fruit it produces. Jesus taught that a tree is known by its fruit: "So, every healthy tree bears good fruit, but the diseased tree bears bad fruit. A healthy tree cannot bear bad fruit, nor can a diseased tree bear good fruit" (Matthew 7:17-18). The fruit of a transformed life is characterized by qualities that reflect the nature of Christ, as described in Galatians 5:22-23: "But the fruit of the Spirit is love, joy, peace, patience, kindness, goodness, faithfulness, gentleness, self-control; against such things there is no law."

These qualities are not produced by human effort but by the work of the Spirit in the believer's life. As believers live out biblical principles, the Holy Spirit brings about this fruit, which in turn serves as a testimony to the power of God's Word to transform lives.

The fruit of a transformed life also extends to the impact it has on others. When believers live according to biblical principles, their lives become a witness to those around them, drawing others to Christ.

Matthew 5:16 encourages believers to let their light shine before others: "In the same way, let your light shine before others, so that they may see your good works and give glory to your Father who is in heaven." The visible transformation in the believer's life serves as a powerful testimony to the reality of God's work in the world.

Maintaining a Transformed Life

Maintaining the transformation brought about by biblical principles requires ongoing commitment and vigilance. The Christian life is not a one-time event but a continuous process of growth and renewal. 2 Peter 3:18 exhorts believers to "grow in the grace and knowledge of our Lord and Savior Jesus Christ." This growth involves a continual return to Scripture, prayer, and fellowship, as well as a willingness to confront and repent of sin.

One of the key aspects of maintaining a transformed life is the practice of self-examination. 2 Corinthians 13:5 instructs believers, "Examine yourselves, to see whether you are in the faith. Test yourselves. Or do you not realize this about yourselves, that Jesus Christ is in you?" Regular self-examination helps believers to stay on track in their walk with Christ, identifying areas where they may have strayed from biblical principles and taking corrective action.

Another important aspect is perseverance. The Christian life is often described as a race, and perseverance is necessary to reach the finish line. Hebrews 12:1-2 encourages believers to "run with endurance the race that is set before us, looking to Jesus, the founder and perfecter of our faith." By keeping their eyes fixed on Jesus and relying on His strength, believers can maintain the transformation that biblical principles have brought about in their lives.

The Eternal Perspective of Transformation

Finally, the transformation brought about by biblical principles has an eternal perspective. The changes that occur in the believer's life are not just for this world but have implications for eternity.

APPLYING GOD'S WORD MORE FULLY

Philippians 1:6 offers a promise of the ongoing work of transformation: "And I am sure of this, that he who began a good work in you will bring it to completion at the day of Jesus Christ." The transformation that begins in this life will be brought to its full completion in the life to come, when believers are made perfect in the presence of God.

This eternal perspective gives meaning and purpose to the process of transformation. 1 Corinthians 15:58 encourages believers to "be steadfast, immovable, always abounding in the work of the Lord, knowing that in the Lord your labor is not in vain." The effort put into living out biblical principles is not wasted but has lasting value in God's kingdom.

In conclusion, the transformation of a believer's life through biblical principles is a profound and ongoing process that begins with a new identity in Christ and is sustained by the power of the Holy Spirit. Through the application of Scripture, prayer, fellowship, and service, believers are gradually conformed to the image of Christ, producing fruit that testifies to the reality of God's work in their lives. This transformation has eternal significance, as it prepares believers for the day when they will be made perfect in the presence of their Savior.

CHAPTER 10 How Can We Find Peace in a World of Anxiety?

The Prevalence of Anxiety in the Modern World

Anxiety has become a pervasive issue in today's society, affecting people from all walks of life. The pressures of modern living, including economic uncertainties, social challenges, health concerns, and global instability, contribute to an environment where anxiety can easily take root. For Christians, finding peace in such a world can seem daunting, but the Scriptures offer both comfort and practical guidance for navigating these turbulent waters.

Anxiety is not a new phenomenon. The Bible speaks extensively about the human condition and the worries that often accompany it. In Job 3:25, we read, "For the thing that I fear comes upon me, and what I dread befalls me." This verse reflects the deep-seated fears that can plague the human heart, leading to anxiety. Yet, the Bible also provides a clear path to peace, grounded in a relationship with Jehovah and a deep trust in His sovereignty.

The Biblical Definition of Peace

Peace, as defined in the Bible, goes far beyond the absence of conflict or worry. The Hebrew word for peace, "shalom," encompasses a sense of completeness, wholeness, and well-being. It is a state of harmony with God, with others, and within oneself. This peace is not dependent on external circumstances but is rooted in the character and promises of God.

In Isaiah 26:3, the prophet declares, "You keep him in perfect peace whose mind is stayed on you, because he trusts in you." This verse emphasizes that true peace is found in focusing on God and trusting in His care and provision. It is a peace that transcends understanding, as Paul describes in Philippians 4:7: "And the peace of God, which surpasses all understanding, will guard your hearts and your minds in Christ Jesus." This peace is a divine gift, guarding the believer's heart and mind against the corrosive effects of anxiety.

Trusting in God's Sovereignty

A key aspect of finding peace in a world of anxiety is trusting in the sovereignty of God. The Bible consistently teaches that Jehovah is in control of all things, orchestrating events according to His perfect will. This knowledge can bring immense comfort, as it assures believers that nothing happens outside of God's providential care.

Proverbs 3:5-6 encourages believers to "Trust in Jehovah with all your heart, and do not lean on your own understanding. In all your ways acknowledge him, and he will make straight your paths." Trusting in God's sovereignty means relinquishing the illusion of control and submitting to His wisdom and plan. It involves acknowledging that God's ways are higher than our ways (Isaiah 55:8-9) and that He works all things together for good for those who love Him (Romans 8:28).

When anxiety arises, it is often because we are focused on circumstances rather than on God's sovereignty. By shifting our focus from our problems to the character of God—His power, wisdom, and love—we can experience a profound sense of peace, knowing that our lives are in His capable hands.

The Role of Prayer in Overcoming Anxiety

Prayer is a powerful tool in overcoming anxiety and finding peace. The Bible repeatedly exhorts believers to bring their concerns and fears to God in prayer, trusting that He hears and cares for them. In 1 Peter 5:7, we are encouraged to "cast all your anxieties on him, because he cares for you." This verse invites believers to offload their burdens onto Jehovah, who is both willing and able to carry them.

Philippians 4:6-7 offers a comprehensive approach to prayer in the face of anxiety: "Do not be anxious about anything, but in everything by prayer and supplication with thanksgiving let your requests be made known to God. And the peace of God, which surpasses all understanding, will guard your hearts and your minds in Christ Jesus." This passage outlines several key principles:

1. **Avoidance of Anxiety**: Believers are instructed not to be anxious about anything, recognizing that anxiety is often a natural human response but one that can be overcome through faith.

2. **Prayer and Supplication**: Believers are encouraged to bring every concern, no matter how small, to God in prayer. Supplication, or earnest pleading, reflects the intensity with which we are to seek God's intervention in our lives.

3. **Thanksgiving**: Gratitude is an essential component of prayer, as it shifts our focus from our problems to God's blessings, fostering a spirit of trust and dependence on Him.

4. **Peace of God**: The result of such prayer is the peace of God, a peace that guards the heart and mind from the assaults of anxiety, providing a supernatural sense of calm in the midst of turmoil.

Through prayer, believers are not only able to communicate their needs to God but also to experience His presence and peace, which dispels anxiety.

The Power of Scripture in Combatting Anxiety

The Word of God is a vital resource for combatting anxiety. Scripture is filled with promises of God's care, provision, and protection, all of which are designed to bring peace to the anxious heart. When believers immerse themselves in Scripture, they fill their minds with God's truth, which counteracts the lies and fears that fuel anxiety.

Psalm 119:165 declares, "Great peace have those who love your law; nothing can make them stumble." Loving God's Word and meditating on it regularly fortifies the believer's heart and mind against the onslaught of anxiety. In times of fear, recalling and meditating on Scripture can provide the strength and reassurance needed to remain steadfast in faith.

One of the most comforting passages for those struggling with anxiety is found in Matthew 6:25-34, where Jesus addresses the worries of life:

"Therefore I tell you, do not be anxious about your life, what you will eat or what you will drink, nor about your body, what you will put on. Is not life more than food, and the body more than clothing? Look at the birds of the air: they neither sow nor reap nor gather into barns, and yet your heavenly Father feeds them. Are you not of more value than they? And which of you by being anxious can add a single hour to his span of life?"

Jesus goes on to assure His followers that God knows their needs and will provide for them, urging them to seek first His kingdom and righteousness. This passage teaches that anxiety is often rooted in a lack of trust in God's provision and encourages believers to focus on God's faithfulness rather than their fears.

The Role of Fellowship in Finding Peace

Christian fellowship plays a significant role in helping believers find peace in a world of anxiety. The community of faith provides encouragement, support, and accountability, all of which are essential for maintaining peace in difficult times. Hebrews 10:24-25 highlights the importance of fellowship: "And let us consider how to stir up one another to love and good works, not neglecting to meet together, as is the habit of some, but encouraging one another, and all the more as you see the Day drawing near."

In fellowship, believers can share their burdens with one another, as instructed in Galatians 6:2: "Bear one another's burdens, and so fulfill the law of Christ." Sharing the struggles of anxiety with trusted brothers and sisters in Christ can provide much-needed support and prayer, helping to alleviate the sense of isolation that often accompanies anxiety.

Moreover, fellowship allows believers to remind one another of God's promises and to encourage each other to trust in His care. Proverbs 12:25 says, "Anxiety in a man's heart weighs him down, but a good word makes him glad." A timely word of encouragement from a fellow believer can lift the burden of anxiety and bring peace to a troubled heart.

The Importance of a Heavenly Perspective

Another key to finding peace in a world of anxiety is maintaining a heavenly perspective. The Bible teaches that this world is not our final home and that the sufferings of this present time are not worth comparing with the glory that is to be revealed to us (Romans 8:18). Keeping an eternal perspective helps to put the challenges and anxieties of life in context, reminding us that our ultimate hope is in the future glory that awaits us in Christ.

Colossians 3:1-2 encourages believers to "seek the things that are above, where Christ is, seated at the right hand of God. Set your minds on things that are above, not on things that are on earth." By focusing on the eternal rather than the temporal, believers can find peace in the knowledge that their present difficulties are temporary and that their future with Christ is secure.

The apostle Peter also speaks to this perspective in 1 Peter 1:6-7: "In this you rejoice, though now for a little while, if necessary, you have been grieved by various trials, so that the tested genuineness of your faith—more precious than gold that perishes though it is tested by fire—may be found to result in praise and glory and honor at the revelation of Jesus Christ." Understanding that trials and anxieties are part of the refining process that prepares us for eternity can bring peace, as it assures us that God is at work even in our struggles.

APPLYING GOD'S WORD MORE FULLY

Practical Steps for Maintaining Peace

While peace is ultimately a gift from God, there are practical steps believers can take to maintain it in their lives. These steps involve both spiritual disciplines and practical actions that align with biblical principles.

Regular Time in God's Word: Immersing oneself in Scripture daily is crucial for maintaining peace. The Word of God renews the mind and fortifies the heart against anxiety. Psalm 119:50 says, "This is my comfort in my affliction, that your promise gives me life." Regular time in God's Word provides the comfort and strength needed to face life's challenges with peace.

Persistent Prayer: As previously discussed, prayer is essential for overcoming anxiety and finding peace. Regular, persistent prayer keeps believers connected to God, allowing them to cast their cares upon Him and receive His peace in return.

Practicing Gratitude: Gratitude shifts the focus from what is lacking to what has been provided, fostering a spirit of contentment and peace. 1 Thessalonians 5:18 instructs, "Give thanks in all circumstances; for this is the will of God in Christ Jesus for you." Practicing gratitude helps to combat anxiety by reminding believers of God's faithfulness and blessings.

Healthy Relationships: Maintaining healthy relationships within the body of Christ provides the support and encouragement needed to navigate anxious times. Ephesians 4:2-3 emphasizes the importance of unity and love in these relationships: "With all humility and gentleness, with patience, bearing with one another in love, eager to maintain the unity of the Spirit in the bond of peace."

Rest and Care for the Body: Taking care of one's physical body is also important for maintaining peace. Jesus Himself recognized the need for rest, as seen in Mark 6:31: "And he said to them, 'Come away by yourselves to a desolate place and rest a while.'" Ensuring adequate rest, exercise, and nutrition can help to reduce anxiety and promote peace.

Edward D. Andrews

The Example of Jesus in Finding Peace

Jesus is the ultimate example of finding peace in a world of anxiety. Throughout His ministry, Jesus faced immense pressure, opposition, and ultimately, the cross. Yet, He remained at peace, fully trusting in His Father's will. In John 14:27, Jesus offers His peace to His disciples: "Peace I leave with you; my peace I give to you. Not as the world gives do I give to you. Let not your hearts be troubled, neither let them be afraid." The peace that Jesus offers is unlike any peace the world can provide—it is a peace rooted in the presence and promises of God.

In Gethsemane, as Jesus faced the imminent suffering of the cross, He turned to prayer, seeking strength and peace from His Father. Luke 22:41-44 records this moment: "And he withdrew from them about a stone's throw, and knelt down and prayed, saying, 'Father, if you are willing, remove this cup from me. Nevertheless, not my will, but yours, be done.' And there appeared to him an angel from heaven, strengthening him. And being in agony he prayed more earnestly; and his sweat became like great drops of blood falling down to the ground."

Jesus' example teaches us that even in the most intense moments of anxiety, peace can be found through prayer and submission to God's will. His reliance on the Father and His ultimate surrender to the cross demonstrate the profound peace that comes from trusting in God's sovereign plan.

In conclusion, finding peace in a world of anxiety is possible through a deep trust in God's sovereignty, a commitment to prayer and Scripture, the support of Christian fellowship, and the practice of gratitude and healthy living. By following the example of Jesus and relying on the power of the Holy Spirit, believers can experience the peace of God that surpasses all understanding, even in the midst of life's most challenging circumstances.

APPLYING GOD'S WORD MORE FULLY

CHAPTER 11 Cultivating Joy and Contentment in Christ

Understanding the Source of True Joy and Contentment

Joy and contentment are central themes in the Christian life, but they are often misunderstood or sought after in the wrong places. The world offers fleeting happiness based on circumstances, material possessions, and temporary pleasures. However, true joy and contentment, as defined by Scripture, are rooted in a relationship with Jesus Christ and are independent of external circumstances.

The Bible presents joy as a deep-seated sense of well-being that comes from knowing and trusting in Jehovah. In Psalm 16:11, David writes, "You make known to me the path of life; in your presence there is fullness of joy; at your right hand are pleasures forevermore." This verse highlights that true joy is found in the presence of God and in a life lived according to His will. It is a joy that is complete and overflowing, not dependent on the ups and downs of life.

Contentment, on the other hand, is the state of being satisfied with what God has provided, trusting that He knows what is best for us. The apostle Paul speaks of this contentment in Philippians 4:11-13: "Not that I am speaking of being in need, for I have learned in whatever situation I am to be content. I know how to be brought low, and I know how to abound. In any and every circumstance, I have learned the secret of facing plenty and hunger, abundance and need. I can do all things through him who strengthens me." Paul's contentment was not tied to his material circumstances but to his reliance on Christ, who gave him the strength to endure all things.

The Role of Trust in Cultivating Joy and Contentment

A critical factor in cultivating joy and contentment is trust in God's sovereignty and goodness. Anxiety and discontent often arise when we doubt God's provision or when we compare our lives to those of others. However, when we trust that Jehovah is in control and that He is working all things for our good (Romans 8:28), we can rest in the assurance that we lack nothing that we truly need.

Proverbs 3:5-6 offers this counsel: "Trust in Jehovah with all your heart, and do not lean on your own understanding. In all your ways acknowledge him, and he will make straight your paths." Trusting God involves surrendering our own desires and plans to His will, believing that He knows what is best for us. This trust is the foundation of both joy and contentment because it frees us from the need to control our circumstances and allows us to find peace in God's provision.

Moreover, trusting in God's goodness helps us to see His blessings in every situation. James 1:17 reminds us that "every good gift and every perfect gift is from above, coming down from the Father of lights with whom there is no variation or shadow due to change." Recognizing that every good thing in our lives is a gift from God leads to a heart of gratitude, which is a key component of contentment.

The Joy of Salvation as the Anchor of Contentment

One of the most profound sources of joy and contentment for believers is the assurance of salvation. The Bible teaches that through faith in Jesus Christ, believers are forgiven of their sins, reconciled to God, and granted eternal life. This assurance is a wellspring of joy that transcends any earthly circumstance.

In Luke 10:20, Jesus tells His disciples, "Nevertheless, do not rejoice in this, that the spirits are subject to you, but rejoice that your names are written in heaven." The joy of knowing that we are saved and that our names are written in the Book of Life is a joy that cannot be taken away, no matter what trials or difficulties we face in this life.

This joy is also tied to our identity in Christ. As children of God, we are loved, accepted, and secure in His hands. Romans 8:38-39 offers a powerful reminder of this truth: "For I am sure that neither death nor life, nor angels nor rulers, nor things present nor things to come, nor powers, nor height nor depth, nor anything else in all creation, will be able to separate us from the love of God in Christ Jesus our Lord." This unshakable love is the foundation of our contentment, as it assures us that we are never alone and that nothing can separate us from God's care.

The Role of Gratitude in Cultivating Contentment

Gratitude is a powerful antidote to discontentment and a key to cultivating joy. The Bible consistently encourages believers to be thankful in all circumstances, recognizing that gratitude shifts our focus from what we lack to what we have been given.

In 1 Thessalonians 5:18, Paul exhorts, "Give thanks in all circumstances; for this is the will of God in Christ Jesus for you." Gratitude is not just a response to good circumstances; it is a deliberate choice to acknowledge God's goodness and faithfulness in every situation. When we practice gratitude, we open our hearts to joy, as we begin to see God's hand at work in our lives and to appreciate the blessings we often take for granted.

Gratitude also fosters contentment by helping us to recognize that God's provision is sufficient. In Philippians 4:6-7, Paul connects gratitude with the peace of God: "Do not be anxious about anything, but in everything by prayer and supplication with thanksgiving let your requests be made known to God. And the peace of God, which surpasses all understanding, will guard your hearts and your minds in Christ Jesus." When we approach God with a thankful heart, even in the midst of trials, we experience His peace and contentment, knowing that He is in control.

The Power of Contentment in the Midst of Trials

One of the most challenging aspects of cultivating joy and contentment is doing so in the midst of trials. The Bible does not promise a life free from difficulties; in fact, Jesus assured His followers that they would face trouble in this world (John 16:33). However, the Bible also teaches that it is possible to experience joy and contentment even in the midst of suffering.

James 1:2-4 offers a radical perspective on trials: "Count it all joy, my brothers, when you meet trials of various kinds, for you know that the testing of your faith produces steadfastness. And let steadfastness have its full effect, that you may be perfect and complete, lacking in nothing." This passage teaches that trials are an opportunity for growth and maturity in faith, and that they can produce a deeper, more resilient joy that is not dependent on circumstances.

Paul also speaks of finding contentment in suffering. In 2 Corinthians 12:9-10, he shares how God's grace was sufficient for him in the midst of his weaknesses: "But he said to me, 'My grace is sufficient for you, for my power is made perfect in weakness.' Therefore I will boast all the more gladly of my weaknesses, so that the power of Christ may rest upon me. For the sake of Christ, then, I am content with weaknesses, insults, hardships, persecutions, and calamities. For when I am weak, then I am strong." Paul's contentment was rooted in the knowledge that God's power was at work in his life, even in his weakest moments, and that his trials were an opportunity for God's strength to be displayed.

The Joy of Serving Others

Another key to cultivating joy and contentment is the joy of serving others. The Bible teaches that true fulfillment is found not in seeking our own interests, but in serving others in love. Jesus Himself modeled this servant-heartedness, as seen in Matthew 20:28: "Even as the Son of Man came not to be served but to serve, and to give his life as a ransom for many."

In Acts 20:35, Paul recalls Jesus' words, "It is more blessed to give than to receive." Serving others shifts our focus from our own needs and desires to the needs of others, which often leads to a greater sense of fulfillment and joy. This joy comes from knowing that we are fulfilling God's purpose for our lives and that we are making a positive impact on the lives of others.

Furthermore, serving others is a practical way to demonstrate our trust in God's provision. When we give of our time, resources, and energy to serve others, we are trusting that God will take care of our needs. This trust fosters contentment, as we learn to rely on God rather than on our own efforts.

Contentment in the Simplicity of Life

The Bible also teaches that contentment is found in simplicity. In a world that constantly promotes the pursuit of more—more possessions, more achievements, more status—the Bible calls believers to a life of simplicity and contentment with what God has provided.

1 Timothy 6:6-8 offers a powerful reminder of the value of contentment: "But godliness with contentment is great gain, for we brought nothing into the world, and we cannot take anything out of the world. But if we have food and clothing, with these we will be content." This passage teaches that true wealth is found not in material possessions but in godliness and contentment. When we learn to be satisfied with the basics of life—food, clothing, and shelter—we free ourselves from the endless pursuit of more and open our hearts to the contentment that comes from trusting in God's provision.

Jesus also taught the importance of simplicity in life. In Matthew 6:19-21, He warns against the dangers of storing up treasures on earth: "Do not lay up for yourselves treasures on earth, where moth and rust destroy and where thieves break in and steal, but lay up for yourselves treasures in heaven, where neither moth nor rust destroys and where thieves do not break in and steal. For where your treasure is, there your heart will be also." By focusing on eternal treasures rather than earthly ones, we cultivate a contentment that is not tied to material wealth but to the eternal riches found in Christ.

The Role of Contentment in Witnessing to the World

Contentment is not only a source of personal joy and peace but also a powerful witness to the world. In a culture that is often driven by discontent and the relentless pursuit of more, a life marked by contentment stands out as a testimony to the sufficiency of Christ.

Philippians 2:14-15 encourages believers to "Do all things without grumbling or disputing, that you may be blameless and innocent, children of God without blemish in the midst of a crooked and twisted generation, among whom you shine as lights in the world." Contentment, expressed through a life free from grumbling and complaining, shines as a light in a world of discontent.

Moreover, a contented life points others to the source of true fulfillment. When people see that our joy and contentment are not dependent on circumstances or material possessions but are rooted in a relationship with Christ, they are drawn to the hope and peace that we have in Him. This opens the door for sharing the gospel and pointing others to the only source of lasting joy and contentment.

In conclusion, cultivating joy and contentment in Christ involves a deep trust in God's sovereignty and goodness, a focus on the joy of salvation, a heart of gratitude, and a commitment to serving others. By embracing simplicity and living a life that reflects the sufficiency of Christ, believers can experience the true joy and contentment that transcends circumstances and stands as a powerful witness to the world.

CHAPTER 12 Practical Steps for Daily Scripture Application

The Necessity of Daily Scripture Application

Daily Scripture application is essential for every believer who desires to live a life that is pleasing to Jehovah. The Bible is not merely a book of historical narratives or moral teachings; it is the living Word of God, intended to transform our lives. Hebrews 4:12 emphasizes the active role of Scripture: "For the word of God is living and active, sharper than any two-edged sword, piercing to the division of soul and of spirit, of joints and of marrow, and discerning the thoughts and intentions of the heart." This verse underscores the power of God's Word to penetrate the deepest parts of our being, revealing and correcting our innermost thoughts and desires.

Applying Scripture daily involves more than just reading the Bible; it requires intentional action, a commitment to integrate its teachings into every aspect of our lives. James 1:22 exhorts, "But be doers of the word, and not hearers only, deceiving yourselves." The goal of daily Scripture application is to move beyond intellectual knowledge to a life that reflects the principles and commands of God's Word.

The Importance of Preparation and Planning

The first practical step in daily Scripture application is preparation and planning. Just as we plan for other important activities in our lives, we must also plan to engage with God's Word meaningfully. This involves setting aside dedicated time each day to read, study, and meditate on Scripture. Without intentionality, the pressures of daily life can easily crowd out our time with God's Word.

In Mark 1:35, we see the example of Jesus, who prioritized time with His Father: "And rising very early in the morning, while it was still dark, he departed and went out to a desolate place, and there he prayed." Jesus' example teaches us the importance of setting aside time, free from distractions, to focus on God. Whether it's early in the morning or another time during the day, establishing a routine for engaging with Scripture is crucial for consistent application.

Planning also involves setting goals for Scripture application. This could include selecting specific passages to study, identifying areas of life that need transformation, or committing to memorizing key verses that address particular struggles or areas of growth. Proverbs 16:3 advises, "Commit your work to Jehovah, and your plans will be established." By committing our plans for Scripture application to God, we invite His guidance and blessing on our efforts.

Reading with Intent: The Key to Effective Application

Reading Scripture with intent is critical to effective application. This means approaching the Bible with a purpose, seeking to understand not just the words on the page but also their meaning and implications for our lives. One way to read with intent is to ask questions of the text, such as: What does this passage reveal about God's character? How does this truth apply to my current situation? What actions should I take in response to this teaching?

Psalm 119:18 serves as a prayer for intentional reading: "Open my eyes, that I may behold wondrous things out of your law." Asking God to open our eyes to the truths of His Word prepares our hearts to receive and apply His teachings. Intentional reading also involves paying attention to the context of the passage, understanding the author's intent, and discerning the timeless principles that apply to our lives today.

One effective method of reading with intent is the inductive Bible study approach, which involves three steps: observation, interpretation, and application. Observation focuses on what the text says, interpretation seeks to understand what the text means, and application considers how the text applies to our lives. This method helps ensure that our application is grounded in a proper understanding of the Scripture.

Meditation: Internalizing God's Word

Meditation on Scripture is another practical step for daily application. Meditation involves pondering and reflecting on God's Word, allowing it to sink deeply into our hearts and minds. This practice is not merely about reciting verses but about internalizing the truths of Scripture so that they shape our thoughts, attitudes, and actions.

Joshua 1:8 emphasizes the importance of meditation: "This Book of the Law shall not depart from your mouth, but you shall meditate on it day and night, so that you may be careful to do according to all that is written in it. For then you will make your way prosperous, and then you will have good success." Meditation on God's Word is linked to obedience and success in living according to His will.

Meditation can take various forms, such as memorizing Scripture, praying through a passage, or journaling thoughts and insights gained from the text. The goal is to keep God's Word at the forefront of our minds throughout the day, allowing it to guide our decisions and actions. Psalm 1:2 describes the blessed person whose "delight is in the law of Jehovah, and on his law he meditates day and night." This continual meditation fosters a life that is rooted and grounded in God's truth.

Practical Application in Daily Decisions

Applying Scripture to daily decisions is where the transformative power of God's Word is most evident. The Bible provides principles and commands that guide us in making choices that honor God. Whether we are facing significant life decisions or everyday choices, Scripture offers wisdom and direction.

Proverbs 3:5-6 provides a foundational principle for decision-making: "Trust in Jehovah with all your heart, and do not lean on your own understanding. In all your ways acknowledge him, and he will make straight your paths." This passage reminds us to rely on God's wisdom rather than our own, seeking His guidance in every decision. By aligning our choices with God's Word, we demonstrate our trust in His sovereignty and goodness.

When facing a decision, it is helpful to ask: What does God's Word say about this situation? Are there specific commands or principles that apply? How will this decision impact my relationship with God and others? By filtering our decisions through the lens of Scripture, we ensure that our actions are in line with God's will.

For example, when making financial decisions, the Bible provides guidance on stewardship, generosity, and contentment. 1 Timothy 6:17-19 instructs believers to "set their hopes on God, who richly provides us with everything to enjoy. They are to do good, to be rich in good works, to be generous and ready to share, thus storing up treasure for themselves as a good foundation for the future." Applying these principles helps us make decisions that reflect our trust in God's provision and our commitment to using our resources for His glory.

Overcoming Obstacles to Scripture Application

Applying Scripture daily is not without challenges. Various obstacles can hinder our efforts, including busyness, distractions, spiritual apathy, and doubt. However, recognizing these obstacles and addressing them with practical strategies can help us remain faithful in applying God's Word.

One common obstacle is busyness. The demands of work, family, and other responsibilities can easily crowd out time for Scripture application. To overcome this, it is important to prioritize time with God's Word and establish a routine that works within our schedule. This might involve waking up earlier, setting aside specific times during the day, or finding creative ways to incorporate Scripture into our daily activities, such as listening to an audio Bible during commutes.

Distractions are another challenge. In our digital age, the constant barrage of notifications, emails, and social media can easily pull our attention away from God's Word. To combat distractions, consider creating a designated space and time for Scripture application, free from interruptions. Additionally, setting boundaries with technology, such as turning off notifications during Bible study, can help maintain focus.

Spiritual apathy, or a lack of motivation, can also hinder Scripture application. When we find ourselves in a spiritual dry season, it is important to remind ourselves of the importance of God's Word and the life-giving power it holds. Praying for renewed passion and asking God to reignite our desire for His Word can help overcome apathy. Psalm 119:36-37 is a helpful prayer in this regard: "Incline my heart to your testimonies, and not to selfish gain! Turn my eyes from looking at worthless things; and give me life in your ways."

Doubt, whether in the reliability of Scripture or in our ability to apply it, can also be a significant obstacle. To address doubt, it is important to study Scripture with a humble heart, seeking to understand God's truth and asking for the Holy Spirit's guidance. 2 Timothy 3:16-17 reassures us of the reliability and usefulness of Scripture: "All Scripture is breathed out by God and profitable for teaching, for reproof, for correction, and for training in righteousness, that the man of God may be complete, equipped for every good work." By trusting in the authority of God's Word, we can confidently apply it to our lives.

Community Support in Scripture Application

Another practical step in daily Scripture application is seeking community support. The Christian life is not meant to be lived in isolation; we are part of the body of Christ, and our growth in applying Scripture is strengthened through fellowship with other believers.

Hebrews 10:24-25 emphasizes the importance of community in the Christian life: "And let us consider how to stir up one another to love and good works, not neglecting to meet together, as is the habit of some, but encouraging one another, and all the more as you see the Day drawing near." Engaging in regular fellowship with other believers provides encouragement, accountability, and the opportunity to learn from one another's experiences in applying Scripture.

Small groups, Bible studies, and discipleship relationships are valuable contexts for sharing insights, discussing challenges, and praying for one another as we seek to apply God's Word. Proverbs 27:17 states, "Iron sharpens iron, and one man sharpens another." In community, we sharpen one another in our understanding and application of Scripture, helping each other grow in faith and obedience.

The Role of Prayer in Scripture Application

Prayer is a vital component of daily Scripture application. As we engage with God's Word, prayer helps us to align our hearts with His will, seek His guidance in understanding and applying Scripture, and rely on His strength to live out His commands.

Psalm 119:33-34 is a prayer for understanding and obedience: "Teach me, O Jehovah, the way of your statutes; and I will keep it to the end. Give me understanding, that I may keep your law and observe it with my whole heart." This prayer reflects a heart that desires not only to know God's Word but also to live it out fully.

Incorporating prayer into our Scripture application can involve praying before, during, and after our time in the Word. Before reading, we can ask God to open our hearts and minds to receive His truth. During our study, we can pray for clarity, wisdom, and insight into the text. After reading, we can pray for the strength to apply what we have learned and for God's guidance in specific areas of our lives.

Prayer also helps us to remain dependent on God's grace as we seek to apply His Word. Philippians 2:12-13 reminds us that while we are called to work out our salvation with fear and trembling, it is ultimately God who works in us "both to will and to work for his good pleasure." Through prayer, we acknowledge our need for God's help in living out His Word and trust in His power to transform our lives.

Continual Growth in Scripture Application

Finally, daily Scripture application is a lifelong journey of growth and transformation. As we consistently apply God's Word, we are gradually conformed to the image of Christ, growing in holiness and maturity.

2 Peter 3:18 encourages believers to "grow in the grace and knowledge of our Lord and Savior Jesus Christ." This growth is a continual process, requiring diligence, perseverance, and a commitment to ongoing learning and application. Each day presents new opportunities to apply God's Word in different areas of our lives, whether in our relationships, work, decisions, or personal struggles.

To sustain continual growth, it is helpful to regularly evaluate our progress in Scripture application. Reflecting on questions such as: How has God's Word transformed my thinking and behavior? In what areas do I still need to grow? How can I deepen my understanding and application of Scripture? can help us stay focused on our spiritual growth.

Additionally, seeking feedback from trusted mentors or spiritual leaders can provide valuable insights and encouragement in our journey of Scripture application. Proverbs 19:20 advises, "Listen to advice and accept instruction, that you may gain wisdom in the future." By remaining teachable and open to correction, we position ourselves for ongoing growth in applying God's Word.

In conclusion, daily Scripture application involves intentional preparation, purposeful reading, meditation, practical decision-making, overcoming obstacles, community support, and continual growth through prayer and reflection. By taking these practical steps, believers can live out the transformative power of God's Word, experiencing the fullness of life that He intends for His children.

CHAPTER 13 Maintaining Spiritual Growth Over the Long Term

The Importance of Long-Term Spiritual Growth

Maintaining spiritual growth over the long term is crucial for every believer who seeks to live a life that reflects the character and will of Jehovah. Spiritual growth is not a one-time event but a lifelong process that requires continuous effort, commitment, and reliance on God's grace. The apostle Paul emphasized the importance of ongoing growth in Philippians 3:12-14, where he writes, "Not that I have already obtained this or am already perfect, but I press on to make it my own, because Christ Jesus has made me his own. Brothers, I do not consider that I have made it my own. But one thing I do: forgetting what lies behind and straining forward to what lies ahead, I press on toward the goal for the prize of the upward call of God in Christ Jesus."

Paul's words remind us that spiritual growth is a journey, one that requires perseverance and a focus on the ultimate goal of being conformed to the image of Christ. This chapter will explore the practical steps and biblical principles that can help believers maintain spiritual growth over the long term, ensuring that their faith remains strong and vibrant throughout their lives.

The Foundation of Spiritual Growth: A Personal Relationship with God

At the heart of long-term spiritual growth is a deep, personal relationship with God. This relationship is the foundation upon which all spiritual growth is built. Jesus emphasized the importance of this relationship in John 15:5, where He declares, "I am the vine; you are the branches. Whoever abides in me and I in him, he it is that bears much fruit, for apart from me you can do nothing." The imagery of the vine and branches highlights the vital connection between the believer and Christ, a connection that must be maintained for spiritual growth to occur.

To cultivate and sustain this relationship, believers must prioritize time with God through prayer, Scripture reading, and meditation. Psalm 1:2-3 describes the blessed person who "delights in the law of Jehovah, and on his law he meditates day and night. He is like a tree planted by streams of water that yields its fruit in its season, and its leaf does not wither. In all that he does, he prospers." Just as a tree needs a constant supply of water to thrive, believers need a constant connection to God through His Word and prayer to grow spiritually.

Prayer is essential in maintaining this connection. It is through prayer that believers communicate with God, express their dependence on Him, and seek His guidance. Philippians 4:6-7 encourages believers to "not be anxious about anything, but in everything by prayer and supplication with thanksgiving let your requests be made known to God. And the peace of God, which surpasses all understanding, will guard your hearts and your minds in Christ Jesus." Regular, intentional prayer keeps the believer's heart aligned with God's will and provides the strength needed to persevere in spiritual growth.

The Role of the Holy Spirit in Spiritual Growth

While believers are called to actively pursue spiritual growth, it is important to recognize that this growth is ultimately the work of the Holy Spirit. The Holy Spirit plays a crucial role in transforming the believer's life, guiding them into all truth, and producing the fruit of the Spirit. In Galatians 5:22-23, Paul lists the fruit of the Spirit: "But the fruit of the Spirit is love, joy, peace, patience, kindness, goodness, faithfulness, gentleness, self-control; against such things there is no law."

These qualities are evidence of the Holy Spirit's work in the believer's life and are the result of ongoing spiritual growth. However, this growth requires the believer's cooperation with the Holy Spirit, which includes yielding to His leading, obeying God's Word, and resisting the desires of the flesh. Galatians 5:16 instructs, "But I say, walk by the Spirit, and you will not gratify the desires of the flesh." Walking by the Spirit means living in daily dependence on Him, allowing Him to guide our thoughts, words, and actions.

The process of sanctification, or being made holy, is a lifelong work of the Holy Spirit in the believer's life. Philippians 1:6 offers assurance of this ongoing work: "And I am sure of this, that he who began a good work in you will bring it to completion at the day of Jesus Christ." The believer's role is to cooperate with the Holy Spirit, trusting that He will continue to work in their life, shaping them into the likeness of Christ.

The Necessity of Spiritual Disciplines

Spiritual disciplines are practices that believers engage in to cultivate their relationship with God and promote spiritual growth. These disciplines include prayer, fasting, Bible study, meditation, worship, and service. While these practices do not earn God's favor, they are means by which believers position themselves to receive God's grace and grow in their faith.

One of the most important spiritual disciplines is the study of Scripture. The Bible is God's revelation to humanity, and it is through the study of Scripture that believers come to know God more deeply and understand His will for their lives. 2 Timothy 3:16-17 emphasizes the importance of Scripture: "All Scripture is breathed out by God and profitable for teaching, for reproof, for correction, and for training in righteousness, that the man of God may be complete, equipped for every good work." Regular study of God's Word equips believers to grow in their faith and to live according to God's will.

Fasting is another important spiritual discipline that can enhance spiritual growth. Fasting is the practice of abstaining from food (or other things) for a period of time to focus on prayer and seeking God. In Matthew 6:16-18, Jesus gives instructions on fasting, emphasizing that it should be done with sincerity and not for the approval of others.

Fasting helps believers to discipline their bodies, to focus on their dependence on God, and to seek His guidance and strength.

Worship is also a crucial discipline for maintaining spiritual growth. Worship is not just an activity that takes place on Sundays; it is a lifestyle of honoring God in every aspect of life. Romans 12:1 urges believers to "present your bodies as a living sacrifice, holy and acceptable to God, which is your spiritual worship." True worship involves surrendering our lives to God, living in a way that pleases Him, and acknowledging His lordship over all areas of life.

Service is another discipline that fosters spiritual growth. Serving others in love reflects the character of Christ and helps believers to grow in humility, compassion, and selflessness. Galatians 5:13 encourages believers to "serve one another in love." Through service, believers grow in their understanding of what it means to follow Christ, who "came not to be served but to serve" (Matthew 20:28).

Perseverance in the Face of Trials

Long-term spiritual growth requires perseverance, especially in the face of trials. The Bible makes it clear that believers will face challenges and difficulties in this life, but it also promises that these trials can be used by God to strengthen faith and promote growth.

James 1:2-4 offers a perspective on trials that is counterintuitive to the world's thinking: "Count it all joy, my brothers, when you meet trials of various kinds, for you know that the testing of your faith produces steadfastness. And let steadfastness have its full effect, that you may be perfect and complete, lacking in nothing." Trials are opportunities for spiritual growth, as they test and refine the believer's faith, producing perseverance and maturity.

Romans 5:3-5 also speaks to the role of trials in spiritual growth: "Not only that, but we rejoice in our sufferings, knowing that suffering produces endurance, and endurance produces character, and character produces hope, and hope does not put us to shame, because God's love has been poured into our hearts through the Holy Spirit who has been given to us." This passage teaches that trials are not meaningless; they have a purpose in God's plan for our growth. Endurance through trials builds character, and this character, in turn, strengthens our hope in God.

To persevere through trials, believers must keep their eyes fixed on Jesus, who is both the source and the goal of our faith. Hebrews 12:1-2 encourages believers to "run with endurance the race that is set before us, looking to Jesus, the founder and perfecter of our faith, who for the joy that was set before him endured the cross, despising the shame, and is seated at the right hand of the throne of God." By focusing on Christ and the hope of eternal life with Him, believers can endure trials with a steadfast faith, knowing that God is using them to accomplish His purposes.

The Role of Community in Spiritual Growth

Spiritual growth is not a solitary journey; it is a communal one. The Bible teaches that believers are part of the body of Christ, and it is within this community that we are encouraged, supported, and held accountable in our spiritual growth.

Hebrews 10:24-25 emphasizes the importance of community in spiritual growth: "And let us consider how to stir up one another to love and good works, not neglecting to meet together, as is the habit of some, but encouraging one another, and all the more as you see the Day drawing near." Regular fellowship with other believers provides opportunities for mutual encouragement, prayer, and support in the journey of faith.

Ecclesiastes 4:9-10 illustrates the strength that comes from community: "Two are better than one, because they have a good reward for their toil. For if they fall, one will lift up his fellow. But woe to him who is alone when he falls and has not another to lift him up!" In the body of Christ, believers are called to bear one another's burdens (Galatians 6:2), to pray for one another (James 5:16), and to build one another up in the faith (1 Thessalonians 5:11).

Discipleship and mentorship are also important aspects of community that contribute to long-term spiritual growth. Paul's relationship with Timothy provides a model of discipleship, where the older, more mature believer invests in the spiritual growth of the younger believer. In 2 Timothy 2:2, Paul instructs Timothy, "And what you have heard from me in the presence of many witnesses entrust to faithful men, who will be able to teach others also." This principle of passing on the faith through discipleship ensures that spiritual growth is sustained and multiplied within the community.

Continual Dependence on God's Grace

Maintaining spiritual growth over the long term requires a continual dependence on God's grace. Spiritual growth is not something we achieve by our own strength or effort; it is the result of God's work in our lives, and it requires our ongoing reliance on Him.

John 15:4-5 emphasizes the necessity of abiding in Christ for spiritual growth: "Abide in me, and I in you. As the branch cannot bear fruit by itself, unless it abides in the vine, neither can you, unless you abide in me. I am the vine; you are the branches. Whoever abides in me and I in him, he it is that bears much fruit, for apart from me you can do nothing." Abiding in Christ involves staying connected to Him through prayer, Scripture, and obedience, and recognizing that any growth or fruit in our lives comes from His grace and power.

Ephesians 2:8-10 reminds us that our salvation and spiritual growth are gifts of God's grace: "For by grace you have been saved through faith. And this is not your own doing; it is the gift of God, not a result of works, so that no one may boast. For we are his workmanship, created in Christ Jesus for good works, which God prepared beforehand, that we should walk in them." God's grace not only saves us but also empowers us to grow and to live out the good works He has prepared for us.

Prayer is a vital way in which we express our dependence on God's grace. In prayer, we acknowledge our need for God's help and ask Him to strengthen us in our walk with Him. Colossians 4:2 encourages believers to "continue steadfastly in prayer, being watchful in it with thanksgiving." Through regular, persistent prayer, we rely on God's grace to sustain and grow us in our faith.

The Hope of Eternal Life as Motivation for Spiritual Growth

Finally, the hope of eternal life with God is a powerful motivation for maintaining spiritual growth over the long term. The Bible teaches that this life is not the end; believers have the promise of eternal life with God, where they will be fully transformed into the likeness of Christ and will enjoy perfect fellowship with Him forever.

1 John 3:2-3 offers this hope: "Beloved, we are God's children now, and what we will be has not yet appeared; but we know that when he appears we shall be like him, because we shall see him as he is. And everyone who thus hopes in him purifies himself as he is pure." The promise of being fully conformed to the image of Christ motivates believers to pursue holiness and spiritual growth in this life.

Titus 2:11-14 also connects the hope of eternal life with the call to live a godly life: "For the grace of God has appeared, bringing salvation for all people, training us to renounce ungodliness and worldly passions, and to live self-controlled, upright, and godly lives in the present age, waiting for our blessed hope, the appearing of the glory of our great God and Savior Jesus Christ, who gave himself for us to redeem us from all lawlessness and to purify for himself a people for his own possession who are zealous for good works." The hope of Christ's return and the fulfillment of His promises encourages believers to live in a way that honors Him, continually growing in their faith and obedience.

In conclusion, maintaining spiritual growth over the long term involves a deep, personal relationship with God, reliance on the Holy Spirit, engagement in spiritual disciplines, perseverance through trials, involvement in a community of believers, continual dependence on God's grace, and the hope of eternal life. By faithfully pursuing these practices and principles, believers can ensure that their spiritual growth is sustained throughout their lives, bringing glory to God and drawing them closer to Him.

CHAPTER 14 Understanding the Holy Spirit and Salvation

The Holy Spirit's Guidance Through Scripture

The Holy Spirit plays a crucial role in guiding believers through the inspired Word of God. As we pray and seek God's direction, it is essential to immerse ourselves in the Scriptures to understand His will. For example, in Psalm 119:105, we read, "Your word is a lamp to my feet and a light to my path." This verse emphasizes the importance of Scripture in providing guidance and clarity in our lives. Just as praying for a job requires taking action by filling out applications, seeking God's guidance through the Holy Spirit involves diligently studying His Word and applying its truths to our circumstances.

The Holy Spirit's Comfort in Times of Distress

The Holy Spirit also provides comfort to believers during times of distress. In 2 Corinthians 1:3-4, Paul writes, "Blessed be the God and Father of our Lord Jesus Christ, the Father of mercies and God of all comfort, who comforts us in all our affliction, so that we may be able to comfort those who are in any affliction, with the comfort with which we ourselves are comforted by God." The comfort we receive from the Holy Spirit equips us to extend that same comfort to others. Engaging with Scripture allows us to understand and experience this divine comfort more deeply.

The Holy Spirit's Role in Conviction and Transformation

The Holy Spirit convicts us of sin and leads us toward transformation through God's Word. John 16:8 says, "And when he comes, he will convict the world concerning sin and righteousness and judgment." This conviction is a call to action, prompting us to align our lives with God's standards as revealed in Scripture. By studying and applying biblical teachings, we can respond to the Holy Spirit's conviction and experience genuine transformation in our lives.

The Holy Spirit's Empowerment for Service

Believers are empowered by the Holy Spirit to serve others and fulfill God's purposes. Acts 1:8 states, "But you will receive power when the Holy Spirit has come upon you, and you will be my witnesses in Jerusalem and in all Judea and Samaria, and to the end of the earth." This empowerment is not passive; it requires us to act upon our prayers and step out in faith. Delving into Scripture helps us understand our calling and equips us to serve effectively in the power of the Holy Spirit.

The Holy Spirit's Guidance in Decision-Making

In times of decision-making, the Holy Spirit provides wisdom and direction through the Scriptures. James 1:5 encourages us, "If any of you lacks wisdom, let him ask of God, who gives generously to all without reproach, and it will be given him." As we pray for wisdom, it is crucial to study God's Word to discern His will. Just as seeking employment involves actively applying for jobs, seeking God's guidance involves diligently searching the Scriptures and applying their principles to our decisions.

The Holy Spirit's Assurance of God's Love

The Holy Spirit assures us of God's love and presence in our lives. Romans 5:5 tells us, "And hope does not put us to shame, because God's love has been poured into our hearts through the Holy Spirit who has been given to us." This assurance strengthens our faith and encourages us to trust in God's promises. Engaging with Scripture reinforces this assurance, helping us to fully grasp and live out the reality of God's love.

The Holy Spirit's Role in Spiritual Growth

Spiritual growth is facilitated by the Holy Spirit through the study and application of Scripture. Galatians 5:22-23 describes the fruit of the Spirit: "But the fruit of the Spirit is love, joy, peace, patience, kindness, goodness, faithfulness, gentleness, self-control; against such things there is no law." These qualities are developed in us as we immerse ourselves in God's Word and allow the Holy Spirit to work in our hearts. Just as praying for personal growth requires intentional effort, spiritual growth necessitates a commitment to studying and living out biblical truths.

The Holy Spirit's Guidance Through the Law

The Holy Spirit guides believers through the law given in the Old Testament. Psalm 119:11 states, "I have stored up your word in my heart, that I might not sin against you." This verse highlights the importance of internalizing Scripture to receive guidance and avoid sin. Just as seeking direction in life involves studying God's commandments, praying for guidance requires actively engaging with and applying the teachings of the law.

The Holy Spirit's Comfort in the Psalms

The Psalms are a rich source of comfort inspired by the Holy Spirit. Psalm 34:18 offers reassurance: "Jehovah is near to the brokenhearted and saves the crushed in spirit." This verse reflects God's comforting presence in times of distress. Engaging with the Psalms allows us to experience the Holy Spirit's comfort, much like actively seeking God's guidance through prayer and study provides solace and direction.

The Holy Spirit's Conviction Through the Prophets

The prophets were inspired by the Holy Spirit to convict Israel of their sins and call them to repentance. Micah 6:8 reminds us, "He has told you, O man, what is good; and what does Jehovah require of you but to do justice, and to love kindness, and to walk humbly with your

God?" This prophetic call to action highlights the role of the Holy Spirit in convicting and guiding believers toward righteous living through Scripture.

The Holy Spirit's Empowerment in Leadership

The Holy Spirit empowers leaders to serve and guide God's people. In Judges 6:34, we read, "But the Spirit of Jehovah clothed Gideon, and he sounded the trumpet, and the Abiezrites were called out to follow him." The Spirit's empowerment of Gideon illustrates the active role of the Holy Spirit in enabling believers to fulfill their God-given tasks. Similarly, our prayers for guidance and strength should be accompanied by actions rooted in Scripture.

The Holy Spirit empowers believers for leadership and service, as seen in the life of Moses. Numbers 11:25 recounts, "Then Jehovah came down in the cloud and spoke to him and took some of the Spirit that was on him and put it on the seventy elders. And as soon as the Spirit rested on them, they prophesied." This empowerment requires us to act upon our prayers and fulfill our God-given responsibilities. Studying the Scriptures equips us for effective leadership under the Holy Spirit's guidance.

The Holy Spirit's Guidance in Times of Uncertainty

In times of uncertainty, the Holy Spirit provides guidance through God's Word. Proverbs 3:5-6 instructs, "Trust in Jehovah with all your heart, and do not lean on your own understanding. In all your ways acknowledge him, and he will make straight your paths." As we pray for direction, it is crucial to seek wisdom from the Scriptures and trust in God's guidance. This active engagement with God's Word helps us navigate life's uncertainties.

The Holy Spirit's Assurance of God's Faithfulness

The Holy Spirit assures us of God's faithfulness, as depicted in Lamentations. Lamentations 3:22-23 proclaims, "The steadfast love of Jehovah never ceases; his mercies never come to an end; they are new every morning; great is your faithfulness." This assurance strengthens our faith and encourages us to rely on God's steadfast love. Delving into Scripture reinforces our understanding of God's faithfulness and helps us trust in His promises.

The Holy Spirit's Role in Teaching and Reminding

The Holy Spirit teaches and reminds us of God's commands, as illustrated in the Old Testament. Nehemiah 9:20 says, "You gave your good Spirit to instruct them and did not withhold your manna from their mouth and gave them water for their thirst." This verse highlights the instructional role of the Holy Spirit in guiding God's people. By immersing ourselves in Scripture, we allow the Holy Spirit to teach and remind us of God's truths, leading us to live in obedience.

Emphasizing the Role of the Holy Spirit

Understanding how we receive illumination and guidance from God is rooted in the inspired, inerrant Word of God. According to 1 Corinthians 2:12-14, the process involves more than merely acquiring a mental grasp of biblical truths; it requires embracing these truths as divinely revealed. The expressions "does not accept," "folly," and "not able to understand" highlight how unbelievers critique and reject divine revelation. This passage does not imply that unbelievers are incapable of understanding the Bible's content; rather, they view it as foolishness. Christians, however, are guided by having the mind of Christ (1 Corinthians 2:16), achieved through being biblically minded. This necessitates a careful analysis of the Bible's genres, historical context, and language, employing the conservative, objective historical-grammatical method of interpretation while avoiding the speculative fallacies of modern biblical criticism.

John 14:16-17; 16:13 Fallacy

The Holy Spirit plays a crucial role in counseling, providing guidance, comfort, and conviction through the Spirit-inspired Word of God. We are guided when we act on behalf of our prayers by digging into the Scriptures and determining what the authors meant by the words they used. To illustrate, if we were praying for a job but never went out and filled out job applications, how would God feel about our prayers? If we were praying about the shame we feel over something, yet we never investigated what the Scriptures had to say about shame so as to apply them, how would Gold feel about our prayer?

What Is Salvation?

The Bible uses the terms "save" and "salvation" in different contexts. Sometimes, they refer to being rescued from physical danger or destruction, like when the Israelites were saved from the Egyptians at the Red Sea (Exodus 14:13-14) or when Paul and others faced peril at sea (Acts 27:20). However, more often, these terms refer to being saved from sin. Since sin leads to death, being saved from sin means having the hope of eternal life (Matthew 1:21; John 3:16-17).

The Bible sometimes speaks of salvation as if it has already been accomplished, even though the full realization of salvation—being completely freed from sin and death—lies in the future (Ephesians 2:5; Romans 13:11).

The Way to Salvation

To be saved, the Bible teaches that you must have faith in Jesus Christ and show that faith by obeying His teachings (Acts 4:10, 12; Romans 10:9-10; Hebrews 5:9). This faith is demonstrated by works—actions that prove your faith is genuine. James 2:24, 26 makes it clear that faith without works is dead, meaning that true faith naturally produces obedience.

However, it's important to understand that these works don't earn salvation. Salvation is a gift from God, given by His grace—His undeserved kindness (Ephesians 2:8-9). This means that while our actions reflect our faith, they do not make us deserving of salvation; rather, God grants it out of His mercy.

APPLYING GOD'S WORD MORE FULLY

Can You Lose Salvation?

Yes, it is possible to lose salvation. Just as someone rescued from drowning could fall back into the water, a person saved from sin could lose their salvation if they stop evidencing their faith. This is why the Bible urges believers to "put up a hard fight for the faith" (Jude 3) and to "keep working out your own salvation with fear and trembling" (Philippians 2:12). This means that Christians must continue to live faithfully and obediently, understanding the serious responsibility of maintaining their salvation.

Who is the Savior—God or Jesus?

The Bible identifies God as the ultimate source of salvation, often referring to Him as "Savior" (1 Samuel 10:19; Isaiah 43:11; Titus 2:10; Jude 25). In the Old Testament, God used various men to deliver Israel from their enemies, and these men were called "saviors" (Nehemiah 9:27; Judges 3:9, 15; 2 Kings 13:5). The same Hebrew word used for these human saviors is also used for Jehovah as the divine Savior (Psalm 7:10).

Jesus is also called "Savior" because God provided salvation from sin through Jesus' sacrifice (Acts 5:31; Titus 1:4). The name "Jesus" itself comes from the Hebrew name "Yehoh·shu′a‘," which means "Jehovah Is Salvation," emphasizing that Jesus is the means by which Jehovah offers salvation to humanity.

Will Everyone Be Saved?

No, not everyone will be saved. Jesus made it clear that while salvation is offered to all, not everyone will accept it. When asked if only a few would be saved, Jesus responded by saying that many would seek to enter the narrow door of salvation but would not be able to (Luke 13:23-24). This indicates that while God desires people to be saved, salvation requires effort and commitment, and some will choose to reject it.

Misconceptions About Universal Salvation

Some believe that the Bible teaches universal salvation, meaning that everyone will be saved regardless of their actions or beliefs. For example, 1 Corinthians 15:22 says, "in the Christ all will be made alive," but the context of this verse is about the resurrection. It means that everyone who is resurrected will have this blessing through Christ, not that everyone will be saved (John 11:25).

Another verse often cited is Titus 2:11, which says that God is "bringing salvation to all people." However, the Greek word translated as "all" can also mean "every kind or variety." This means that God is making salvation available to all sorts of people, regardless of their background or nationality, as seen in Revelation 7:9-10, where people from all nations are saved.

Finally, 2 Peter 3:9 says that God "does not desire anyone to be destroyed." While God wants everyone to be saved, He does not force anyone to accept salvation. His day of judgment will still involve the destruction of those who reject His offer of salvation (2 Peter 3:7).

In summary, salvation is a gift from God, made possible through faith in Jesus Christ and demonstrated by obedient actions. While God desires everyone to be saved, salvation is not automatic and can be lost if faith is not maintained. Not everyone will be saved, as it requires accepting God's provision for salvation and living according to His will.

www.ingramcontent.com/pod-product-compliance
Lightning Source LLC
Chambersburg PA
CBHW022107040426
42451CB00007B/166